Model Letters
and
Memos

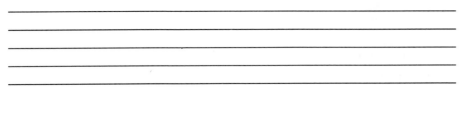

Model Letters
and
Memos

A Handbook for Scientists
and Engineers

Ron Tepper

John Wiley & Sons, Inc.

New York • Chichester • Brisbane • Toronto • Singapore

Note: A disk is contained in this book.
THE PURCHASER MAY MAKE BACKUP COPIES FOR HIS/HER OWN
USE ONLY AND NOT FOR DISTRIBUTION OR RESALE. THE
PUBLISHER ASSUMES NO RESPONSIBILITY FOR ERRORS,
OMISSIONS, OR DAMAGES, INCLUDING WITHOUT LIMITATION
DAMAGES CAUSED BY THE USE OF THE INFORMATION
CONTAINED THEREIN.
REQUIREMENTS:
An IBM, PC Family computer or compatible computer, a 3.5″ high-
density floppy drive, PC DOS, MS-DOS, or DR DOS Version 2.0 or later,
a printer, any ASCII editor or Word Processor.

Library of Congress Cataloging-in-Publication Data:

Tepper, Ron, 1937–
     Model letters and memos : a handbook for scientists and engineers
   / Ron Tepper.
       p.   cm.
     Includes index.
     ISBN 0-471-13917-3 (cloth/disk : alk. paper)
     1. Technical writing—Handbooks, manuals, etc.   2. Letter writing—
   Handbooks, manuals, etc.   I. Title.
   T11.T378   1996
   808′.066651—dc20   95-45547

Printed in the United States of America

10   9   8   7   6   5   4   3   2   1

How to Use the Disk

The diskette requires an IBM-PC or compatible computer with DOS version 2.0 or later. It can be used in both DOS and Windows environments. The files can be read into your word processing software program using the directions given below. If your word processing program is not listed below, you can load these files by following the directions for your particular word processing programs as mentioned in your software manual. Using the index in your software manual, refer to the section on *Importing ASCII files or Loading Documents from Other Word Processors.*

COMPUTER REQUIREMENTS

The enclosed diskette requires an IBM PC or compatible with the following:

IBM PC DOS or MS DOS 2.0

Compatible computer with 256K minimum

A 3.5" double sided, double density drive

Optional equipment includes a DOS compatible printer and a popular word processing package like WordPerfect® or Microsoft® Word for Windows to read and print the letter and memo files.

HOW TO MAKE A BACKUP COPY

Before you start to use this disk, we strongly recommend that you make a backup copy of the original. Making a backup copy of your disk allows you to have a clean set of files saved in case you accidentally change or delete a file. Remember, however, that a backup disk is for your own personal use only. Any other use of the backup disk violates copyright law.

1. Insert your DOS disk into Drive A of your computer.
2. At the A:>, type DISKCOPY A: A: and press Return.

v

You will be prompted by DOS to place the disk to be copied into drive A.

    3. Place Model Letters and Memo's: A Handbook for Scientists and Engineers disk into drive A.

Follow the directions on the screen to complete the copy. When you are through, remove the new copy of the disk and label it immediately. Remove the original disk and store it in a safe place.

HOW TO INSTALL THE DISK

The enclosed diskette contains over 150 data files in a compressed format. In order to use the files, you must run the installation program for the diskette.

    You can install the diskette onto your computer by following these steps:

    1. Insert the *Model Letters and Memo's: A Handbook for Scientists and Engineers* disk into drive A of your computer.

    2. At the A:> type INSTALL and press Return.

Next, you will have the opportunity to name the subdirectory to store the data files. The default subdirectory name is LETTERS.

    To accept this name:

    3. Press Return.

The installation program will proceed to copy the files to your hard disk. When all copying is complete, you can press any key to exit the installation program. Remove the original disk from drive A and store it in a safe place.

GETTING STARTED

The forms on the disk are in ASCII format. ASCII format is a standard text format for DOS computers. Using this format, a number of different users with different word processing programs can read the disk. Once the forms are loaded into your word processor, you can customize them to suit your individual needs.

    This means that regardless of your word processing program (WordPerfect, Word for Windows, WordStar, etc.), you can still use the files on this disk. As an example, following are instructions for reading files into some popular word processing programs.

Reading Files into Wordperfect 5.0

To read the files into WordPerfect 5.0 follow these steps:

1. Load the WordPerfect program as normal.

2. When [Document 1 0 unmodified] appears on screen, select OPEN from the FILE menu.

3. The OPEN dialog will appear. At this box, make the appropriate selections for the drive and subdirectory of the document you want to review. For instance, to open files in the directory, you must first select the LETTERS directory.

4. Under the FILES option on the left side of the dialog box, enter 1-11-L as the file name.

5. The CONVERT FILE FORMAT dialog box will appear on screen with the option for ASCII TEXT (DOS) highlighted. Click OK to proceed.

The file will immediately load into WordPerfect for Windows.

6. To print the file, select PRINT form the FILE menu.

You can make any changes or revisions to the document. When you are through editing it, you can save it under a new file name before you quit.

Reading Files into Microsoft Word for Windows

To read the files into Microsoft Word for Windows, merely follow the steps:

1. Load Word for Windows program as normal.

2. When an Untitled document is displayed, select OPEN from the FILE menu.

3. The OPEN FILE dialog box will appear. Make the appropriate selections, for the drive and subdirectory of the documents. For instance, the files may be located in drive C under directory LETTERS.

4. Under the FILE NAME option on the left side of the dialog box, enter 1-11-L as the file name. If you want to look through a list of files , you must type in *.* under the FILE NAME option. Otherwise, Word for Windows will only look for files with the DOC extension.

5. The CONVERT FILE dialog box will appear on screen with a listing of different file types. Select DOS TEXT WITH LAYOUT as the file type and press OK.

The file will immediately load into Word for Windows.

6. To print the file, select PRINT from the FILE menu.

You can make any changes or revisions to the document. When you are through editing it, you can save it under a new file name before you quit.

Reading the Files into Other Word Processing Programs

To use these files with other word processing programs, refer to the documentation that accompanies your software. Often, the procedure is very similar to those listed above, with two primary steps:

1. Identify the file you want to load from the *Model Letters and Memo's: A Handbook for Scientists and Engineers* disk and indicate the filename to your word processor.

2. Identify the file as a DOS text file.

After these general steps, most word processing will immediately load the file.

USER ASSISTANCE AND INFORMATION

John Wiley & Sons, Inc., is pleased to provide assistance to users of this package. Should you have questions, regarding use of this package, please call our technical support number: (212) 850-6194 between 9:00 AM and 4:00 PM EST, Monday–Friday.

Disk Contents

Preface

The two words information *and* communication *are often used interchangeably, but they signify quite different things. Information is giving out; communication is getting through.*
—Sydney J. Harris

For many people, the thought of writing a simple note, a short letter, or a brief memo is enough to cause trauma. This is especially true of scientists, engineers, and other professionals whose communications with their peers rely on their superb mathematical and analytical skills, their carefully constructed logic, and their detail-oriented research.

They have a store of information, but how can relevant data be communicated in a manner that is understandable—and that takes less time than the research itself?

That's what this book is all about. It will show you—in a simple, practical, how-to manner—ways of communicating effectively, both inside and outside your company, through internal and external memos and short and long letters.

Letter and memo writing is "formulated," that is, made easy for the scientist and engineer. Follow the directions—or the formula—and you are virtually guaranteed to produce correspondence that is easy to read, effective, and communicative.

For example, there are two distinct formulas that readers can utilize. The first formula, developed by mail order copywriters, applies to the technical professions. This four-step process, called AIDA, enables the writer to follow a precise formula and come up—consistently—with correspondence that is lucid and meaningful. AIDA stands for **A**ttention, **I**nterest, **D**esire, **A**ction. With it, complex communiqués are made simple. Letters that previously took hours to write can be written in a fraction of the time. Even if you have never been able to write a well-organized proposal, or have few writing skills, you can use the AIDA approach to ensure clear written communication.

A second formula introduced is IBC (**I**ntroduction, **B**ody, **C**onclusion), which is a remarkable, time-saving tool for both memos and letters. It illustrates, in practical, how-to terms and with examples, exactly how a memo can be written, conclusions developed, and introductions written, in a matter of minutes.

Another writing aid for professionals is unveiled—USP (**U**nique **S**elling **P**roposition). This formula explains why every letter and memo—regardless of what the topic happens to be—is really a sales letter (or memo). By applying USP, letters and memos *communicate and sell.*

This book contains another unique writing aid—two full chapters of boilerplate letters and memos for the scientist, engineer, and professional. These documents were provided by engineers and other technical professionals who are accomplished writers and communicators. Nearly 200 letters and memos covering more than 125 different subjects can be found throughout the book.

In addition, you will find:

- Dozens of hints on how to make your correspondence more effective;

- The use of summaries and where to place them;

- How to handle lengthy documents and make them more readable;

- How to virtually guarantee the recipient will not only read what you write but will understand the message you want to get across.

This comprehensive presentation would not have been possible without the help of many scientists, engineers, and other professionals who generously gave their time and provided memos and letters as guidelines. Thanks to them, this book will not only make effective letter and memo writing easier, but it will save you countless hours in front of the word processor.

RON TEPPER

Acknowledgments

Special thanks to Ken Bergren, Paul Amirpanah, Bob Braun, and William Faust, four accomplished and talented scientific and engineering professionals who contributed enormously to this book. A special acknowledgment to Janet Tepper for her superb help in formatting the book's typographical components.

Contents

Chapter 1

What Makes a Letter or Memo Effective?—12 Rules to Remember

If it is just one page, I promise to read it with attention. If it is longer, my secretary will put it straight into a wastepaper basket.

Sir Winston Churchill

The only thing we have to fear is fear itself.

President Franklin Delano Roosevelt

THE "SOUND BITE" OUTLOOK

Radio news broadcasts seldom devote more than 30 seconds to each story. Anchors on television news shows rarely spend more than 20 seconds introducing a story, and the film clips that depict the event usually run 10 to 20 seconds, rarely longer. Not long ago, most commercials ran 60 seconds. Now, 5-second and 10-second spots can be purchased. We live in a "sound bite" culture. Communication is short and to the point. Messages are rapid-fire. Take 60 seconds to deliver your message, and your audience is asleep or has switched to another channel.

Should true communication take longer? Winston Churchill answered that question succinctly: *No!* If you cannot say something in one page, maybe it is not worth saying at all. Could President Roosevelt's message have been any more potent in 20 words instead of 10?

SHORT IS IN

Today, we have less time for reading—or watching TV—than ever before. People read less, whether they are scientists, engineers, bricklayers, or marketing executives. Everyone wants to see the bottom line—quickly. They want newscasters to get to the point—quickly. Sales of remote control units have flourished, not because people are too lazy to walk to the TV but because the unit allows the viewer to change channels rapidly if someone on the TV screen does not get to the point in 15 or 20 seconds.

The same economy is true of print media. *USA Today* has a circulation of more than a million copies. Its short, to-the-point, capsuled, 250-word news stories have set a successful pattern that other publishers are watching. Nearly every newspaper has jumped on the bandwagon: "capsule" contents of the edition appear up front so that readers can scan the important stories.

Time and *Newsweek* have revamped their layouts; both now offer short, punchy headlines and stories. *Newsweek*, for instance, has "Periscope," a one-page synopsis of some of the week's hottest events. A typical issue may spotlight six or seven stories on just one page. Whether readers are turning the pages of *Newsweek*, *Time*, the *Los Angeles Times*, or the *Chicago Tribune*, they almost always find a 10- or 20-word wrap-up, or capsule summary that they can peruse quickly and get the message without reading the full text.

Despite the efforts of national newsmagazines and daily newspapers to accommodate the fact that short is in, their ranks continue to shrink. Time has become a precious commodity, and no one has time to read lengthy articles. Nightly television gives us the news instead.

When people are impatient with professionally written articles and news, just imagine how much shorter their attention span is when they receive 2- and 3-page letters, or overly long memos. The written word—whether in the form of a letter or a memo—has fallen victim to today's pressures on their time.

AVOID THE RAMBLE

For the professional, engineer, or scientist who wants to get a message across, the first rule is: Deliver it in sound bite fashion. That does *not* mean every letter has to be less than a page, or every memo has to be one paragraph. But, in order to be read, correspondence and memos have to be brief, succinct, and to the point. Every word must count. Try staying with the full text of the following lengthy memo.

From:
To:
Date:

As you may know, a few months ago we completed a study of our engineering facilities, and discovered that there were certain things lacking within our maintenance facilities. Although many of our departments have problems because they are not up-to-date, the maintenance area had glaring deficiencies. For instance, there was not a procedure in place to report the spillage of toxic cleaning compounds. If something happened, it was up to the supervisor to call security, and security would notify engineering, which would dispatch a team to decide if there was anything seriously amiss. If there was, a call would be made, depending upon the seriousness of the spill, to an outside hazardous cleanup team, usually from the _____ company.

Now, we are in the process of upgrading our maintenance area. One of the first things we are going to do is to put a hazardous cleanup team in place 24 hours a day. Thus, if something is spilled at any time, we will have immediate response, whether the spillage is with maintenance or some other department. In putting the hazardous cleanup team together, the suggestion was made that some of our employees are from other industries and they may have had experience in handling materials of this type. If so, and you are interested in becoming a member of the team, contact John _____ at extension 5465.

This memo went on for another page before it was finally concluded. Aside from its wordiness and overly long paragraphs, the writer spent an inordinate amount of time giving background rather than the planned remedy for a bad situation.

What was the purpose of the memo? To generate membership for the hazardous cleanup team that was being organized. The memo failed to answer four key questions:

1. Was this a full-time position?

2. Were people being asked to switch jobs?

3. Was the cleanup volunteer work?

4. Were any benefits planned for those who joined the team?

Realistically, the entire rambling memo could have been condensed into a few paragraphs:

We recently began revamping our maintenance department and examining the procedures that should be followed in the event of a hazardous spill. Management has decided to form a special, round-the-clock hazardous cleanup team, which will respond to any calls relating to spills. There will be two members per team, and they will work standard, 8-hour shifts. They will not be moved from their present assignments, but will be called on in the event a spill occurs on their shift.

In addition to their regular salary, members of the team will be compensated with additional wages calculated at a rate of 15% per hour or fraction of an hour. If you are interested in applying for one of the team positions, contact Human Resources, extension 324.

Notice the difference in the two memos. The first memo gives little information and drags on; the second goes directly to the pertinent facts. All memos and letters should be short and succinct. Today's professionals live in a fast-paced, competitive world where they are accustomed to receiving information in sound bite fashion. Communication inside and outside the corporate world has changed. Long diatribes are out; short, precise messages are in. Whether we are talking engineering or auto repair, brevity and clarity are the keys to effectiveness.

How long is *brief*? The length of a correspondence depends on the message to be conveyed, but keep this rule in mind: a memo longer than one page will lose a large portion of your readers. If your message requires more than one page, then start the document with a summary. Your summary should be one paragraph, consisting of three or four sentences.

GENERALITIES VS. SPECIFICS

Writing in a sound bite style can be difficult. Letters and memos are factual communications. They should not feature an abundance of adjectives, nor should they contain generalizations. Good letters and memos are organized and to the point, do not ramble, and are not loaded with technical jargon. Professionals composing letters or memos must remember that those reading it will not necessarily be proficient at the profession. The CEO of a major corporation may not be familiar with engineering "talk" or acronyms. A funding request memo that is loaded with occupational talk and slang might end up in the CEO's wastepaper basket.

The following memo from an aerospace company is an example of plain language and specific information conveyed in a friendly tone.

If you've noticed that the E-mail with St. Louis is not what it used to be, take heart; improvement is on the way. An upcoming _____ service migration will allow Macintosh-based Microsoft Mail users to communicate with users in St. Louis.

Although the memo is on a technological subject, it is written for everyone to understand.

KEEP IT SIMPLE

In any communication, simplicity is the goal, and occasional humor does not hurt. As a technical professional, you will not write *only* technical memos. Guard against developing two styles: a technical style when your audience is your peers, and a nontechnical style for everyone else. Instead, aim at writing *all* your communications in simple, easy-to-understand language.

Many technically oriented publications are edited by people who do not understand technical jargon. Editors are hired for their ability to clarify ideas, their knowledge of correct expression, and their word skills. Frequently, they know nothing about the technology described, but they are reliable judges of whether it has been given a good description.

If you are writing a letter or an article, or supplying a news release to a technical publication, remember to keep it simple or your message may not be understood. Good news releases should be written on an 8th-grade level. This does not mean that letters and memos should consist entirely of one-syllable words. If you are unsure of your approach, use this question as a guide: "Will the reader understand what I am saying?"

In the past, to be wordy and witty was appreciated. Today, witty is appreciated but wordy is not. Television has pulled us away from books, but it has not diminished the importance of words. In fact, the less we read, the more important each word is. Word choice is critical for the engineer, scientist, or professional trying to convey a message.

Many professionals have difficulty delivering messages with simplicity. The following internal memo from a prominent aerospace company lacks the clarity that simpler language would have given it.

During the planning of this subproject, you were identified as a functional person who would be responsible for the completion of one or more project tasks. Please refer to the project plans for those assigned tasks and related deliverables.

The target completion date for those tasks is shown on the attached schedule. Please review this information and provide any needed corrections by the date in the plan. Your acceptance of this plan and schedule will be assumed if you have not responded by the above date.

Stilted terms such as "functional person" are not needed. Its wordiness makes this memo confusing and vague.

The need for brevity and clear communication goes beyond letters and memos. In any written proposal, that need is critical. Few executives have time to read a 30-page document. For a proposal to be effective, it should begin with an easy-to-read summary that is no longer than a page.

CORRESPONDENCE IS A SALES TOOL

Whether six lines or six pages, all effective letters and memos have one element in common: they sell the reader. The principles that apply to selling products or services also apply to writing.

The sales effort is more obvious in proposals, but it is equally present in correspondence. The common consensus is that letters or memos are intended to inform managers or others within a company, not to sell them anything. But every effective correspondence "sells" something to readers: sells—a point of view, or information, or a product. What could a thank-you note possibly sell? Sincerity; the fact that the writer enjoyed a gift, a helping hand, a party, or whatever.

CORRESPONDENCE CAN BOND

The following note was sent by the vice president of one region to the vice president of another region within the same company.

Dear Jim:

Your hospitality was exceptional, the dinner was incredible, and the information on the new project was invaluable. Although we have both been with _____ Industries for several years, this was the first time we really had a chance to sit down and discuss our problems and projects. The exchange was one of the best I have ever had with anyone in the organization. Frankly, we should be doing this more often, only next time dinner is on me. My sincere thanks for a great evening.

This thank-you note did more than just say thanks. Its tone bonded the relationship between the two vice presidents and opened the way for future communication and information exchange. The thoughtfulness expressed by sending the note and the gratitude conveyed in its wording did a good job of selling Jim on his counterpart's sincerity and desire to meet again. Without the thank-you note, these two divisions may not have attained the increased sales and profitability that developed from this two-way exchange.

Effective letters and memos not only sell, but they use a formula called AIDA (**A**ttention, **I**nterest, **D**esire, **A**ction) which will be examined in depth in Chapter 2. We will also look at another simple letter and memo guide, IBC (**I**ntroduction, **B**ody, **C**onclusion), and how this three-step approach creates more effective writing.

KEY INGREDIENTS

There are 12 key ingredients in making correspondence more effective.

1. Write clearly and then edit, edit, edit! If you have enough time before their delivery, you can increase the impact of letters and memos by putting them away in a drawer for a day. Then reread them, giving special attention to errors or difficult language. The following is an example of how editing can improve communication. This memo was written by an engineer who held it for a day in order to reread it with a fresh eye.

From:
Date:
To: Staff
Subject: Equipment Specifications

In order to ensure that the spray robots, spray equipment, and spray booths in the manufacturing center are properly interfaced, the attached paragraphs should be added to the indicated specifications where applicable. These additions establish the robot vendor as the responsible party for this interfacing.

Also, in response to the referenced memo, the spray and material feed equipment specifications will be turned over to the referenced party by John _____ . These specifications will include similar sections for equipment interfacing.

Finally, functional interfacing requirements will be written for inclusion in the robot specifications. These requirements will also be turned over to you by the engineering organization.

As originally written, the memo was confusing. The message was garbled and difficult to understand because the engineer was writing thoughts instead of providing information. Often, when we know what we want to say, we put it down too quickly, without organizing our thoughts into a coherent flow of information. Confusion results among our readers.

Here is the same memo after editing was done the next day. The wording is now informative and understandable.

> In order to ensure that our spray procedures in manufacturing are working efficiently and together, I have attached some additional operating specifications that should clarify the function of each step in the spray operation. The _____ Company, the robot vendor, will be responsible for resolving any problem that develops with any of these procedures.
>
> Please be aware that the specifications needed for the operation of the spray and material feed equipment are being supplied by John _____ Company.
>
> Specifications for how the robot controller responds when each safety interlock is tripped are in progress. They will be turned over to you by the engineering department, which is responsible for this phase of the operation.
>
> With three different sources providing information, there may be gaps or overlaps. Please contact me if you have any questions.

By breaking the topics into units, dividing their coverage into separate paragraphs, and writing as one would speak, the author of this memo has produced a document that could be understood by anyone.

2. Do not send letters or memos while angry or frustrated. Emotions lead to poorly constructed communications. Calm down, and write the correspondence when your thoughts are clear. Here's an example of a memo that was written and sent during a moment of anger. Its testy wording almost ruined the career of a talented executive.

> Yesterday afternoon, Lani _____ of your department placed a call to our new client, _____ Industries in Honolulu. I distinctly recall telling your department, and you, that contact with this particular firm was something I did not want anyone within our organization to have unless I approved of it first. This is a delicate agreement and the conversations between our two firms must be cleared by me.

The memo was sent to the head of Lani's department, with copies (cc) to the president and division vice president. The tone of the message was poor, but even worse was the fact that the new client had previously called the department and asked Lani for assistance. Lani's boss immediately wrote the following response at the bottom of the memo:

> Sorry about the confusion. But you'd better make the rules clear to Henry _____ , who heads _____ Industries in Honolulu. It seems Henry had called Lani and asked for help. Perhaps next time we should ask Henry to clear the contact through your office.

The document, showing the reply, was copied to everyone who had received the first memo. If you work in today's competitive corporate environment, it would be beneficial to consider these three questions before sending any note or memo.

1. Will I be less angry in 24 hours? If so, I should put this away and wait to see how I feel and what the impact might be.
2. Do I know all the facts?
3. Would it be better to speak to this person face-to-face?

The answer is usually *yes* to the first and third questions and *no* to the second.

3. Write well. Limit the use of adjectives and hype. Support all of your points. If a point cannot be supported, it's probably not valid. The following memo was sent by an anxious executive in need of improved technology.

> We have discussed the purchase of new PCs for technology for the past four months, and needless to say, we all agree that something should be done. Hopefully, purchase the equipment and do it as soon as possible.
>
> Regardless of budget constraints, I can tell you that our department is not functioning at its best because we lack the proper equipment. When we do not do things on a timely basis, this impacts other units, too. I know production has been running behind, and I would venture to say that if we were able to get our equipment, we could supply production much quicker, and they would be able to catch up.
>
> Next Monday, we meet again to discuss capital expenditures, and I will make a motion to purchase the equipment. In the production crunch which we are facing, it makes sense.

The memo states that production is running behind, but the cause of the problem is never mentioned, nor are any facts and figures to support the argument. The excited executive just assumes the predicament will be understood. Assumptions are not valid arguments when you're trying to convince budget committees or senior managers.

4. Spell it right. Typographical errors will ruin the effectiveness of a letter or memo. Typos say the writer did not care enough to check details, and if the letter or memo is not worth a final review, it may not be important enough to read. This example contains only two sentences:

> The enclosed article by President Vaughan is something we can all benefit from. Congratulations to President Vaughn for a well-researched, carefully constructed piece.

While rushing to get the article distributed, this executive misspelled the president's name. Unfortunately, the president was on the distribution list.

5. Make it easy to read. Make your paragraphs short and concise. Shorter paragraphs (two or three sentences) make the correspondence easier to read. Lengthy sentences and paragraphs discourage reading. The following is an example of a long memo.

> The revision within our department will take place on the first Monday of October, and on that day the various departments will switch locations as I indicated on the enclosed floorplan, and they will operate from the new cubicles starting on Tuesday. Telephone connection and reconnection will take place on Monday, with any special needs handled late Monday afternoon by the special crew that the _____ Telephone company is bringing in for the move.
>
> Filing and storage cabinets should be marked by Friday afternoon preceding the move, since the movers will be in the plant over the weekend and plan to have everything moved to your new quarters by Sunday afternoon. The heavy-duty copiers, and other technology equipment that will be used in the new facility, will be moved by the movers over the weekend as well, so they should be clearly marked on Friday afternoon, too.

The length and format of the memo make it confusing. The following revised memo uses bulleted elements and shorter sentences for clarity.

Schedule for our department's move:

- On Friday, Oct. 3, all desks, cabinets, technology equipment, and anything that is to be moved into your new quarters should be marked with the appropriate stamp.

- Telephone equipment should not be marked. Your numbers will be moved, but the equipment stays. Those of you who have special telephone needs—that is, any equipment that is not the standard telephone with three rollovers—will not have your full equipment in place until late Monday, probably after 4 P.M.

- All equipment, aside from file cabinets and desks, will be moved over the weekend.

- Desks and the remainder of the equipment will be moved to the new location by 9 A.M. Monday. Those of you who generally report to work prior to 9 A.M. should rearrange your schedule and plan to report no earlier than 9.

Chronological ordering of each item makes this memo easier to read. The list takes the reader from beginning to end, with no jumping back and forth.

6. Make it neat. Use a letter-quality printer. Your letter or memo should not look like it came out of a manual typewriter that desperately needed a new ribbon.

7. Keep it simple. Do not use jargon and acronyms. The following memo is so full of acronyms that the point is lost.

The graduate BSEE who have served a minimum of six years in the CRI program and five years in ACA are eligible for a special ACA award being presented at the end of the fiscal year by the CES committee.

The first time an acronym is used it should be spelled out, with the initials in parentheses. After that use only the initials. Remember, not everyone will know what the acronym means. To avoid confusion, use the full term unless it is repeated so often that its repetition would be tiresome.

8. Write for the "lowest common denominator." Consider all persons who will receive the letter or memo, and write on a level that the person who knows the least about the subject will understand. This important concept is frequently overlooked, especially in technical professions, because we assume that anyone working in our field or for our company understands all of the jargon. The president of the company may not be familiar with the specific terminology for a project.

9. Tread lightly with interdepartmental correspondence. The following memo was sent from an engineer to the marketing director of a large airplane manufacturing facility. The memo caused quite a stir because of the analysis and the fact that it came from engineering, not marketing. Its content irritated the marketing vice president because the analysis had come from outside his area. But, he later admitted, the engineer had put his finger on the problem.

> I just read that the _____ has very low operating costs. Still, we have fallen far beneath our sales projections. After studying the problem for many months, I have come up with the following, which may explain our sales slump.
>
> 1. Use of crossover crews. It is advantageous to an airline to have several similar aircraft of different sizes that can be flown by the same crew. In the same size, both the _____ and the _____ can be flown by the same crew, and the _____ will have several different sizes eventually that can be flown by the same crew. Our _____ has no current derivative models.
>
> 2. Fears for our company's future. Whether they are true or not, the rumors are running through the aerospace industry. There is constant disruption of positive messages, and prospective customers do not want to purchase equipment from a company that may not be in business very long.
>
> 3. Our engine design. The _____ engine design is not as popular with carriers today, especially with our competitors coming out with more fuel-efficient two-engine models, the _____ and _____ .

The engineer defined and explained the problem in laypersons' terms in just over one page. Some consultants might have submitted a 100-page report, but this engineer attracted management's attention with a brief typewritten document.

The memo gave a problem analysis, not a solution. When engineering suggests to sales what the marketing problems are, there can be resistance. People who have a particular expertise tend to object when someone who lacks that expertise steps on their "turf." Thus, writing a critical memo requires diplomacy. Notice that the engineer did not criticize marketing for failure to sell the airplanes, nor did he point to anyone within the engine design department, although his inference is clear.

Diverse departments within all major companies may have similar problems. Although there are exceptions, no one wants someone in another area telling them what's wrong and how to solve it. Thus, Rule number 9: Tread lightly with internal correspondence, especially if you are trying to solve problems, or point out why there is a problem.

10. Think about the audience before you write. Jay Abraham, a successful copywriter and direct-mail entrepreneur, maintains that the key to any successful letter or memo is the writer's ability to keep the recipient in mind. Abraham suggests asking the following questions before you begin writing:

- What will interest them (your audience)?
- How should it be said?
- How can I get the message across so they will remember it?

Chase Revel, founder of *Entrepreneur Magazine,* advises those writing correspondence to always keep in mind that "we are motivated by our self-interests. That may sound blunt, but it is true. Nearly always, people want to do what is best for themselves. If you can convince the recipients that your course of action or suggestion is best, you can win them over. Remember, too, that we are all motivated by some basic instincts—ego and greed. The most successful direct-mail solicitations play upon those two motivations. And, the most impactful letters and memos, whether they are selling something or not, will play upon those emotions, too."

Abraham supplied the following letter opening, which, although a sales pitch and not regular correspondence, is a good example of the emotions a letter can evoke:

Dear Friend:
    I'd like to take a minute of your time to talk about an extremely important subject: your health!

This opening would get nearly everyone's attention. (In Chapter 2, we will examine this attention-getting device.) The same device could be used in engineering or scientific letters. Imagine a company letter or memo that opened this way:

I'd like to take a moment of your time to discuss something we all believe to be important: our jobs.

That attention-getting lead sentence can be attached to a request for equipment, additional help, change in operations, or more funding.

11. Keep the three "Ps" in mind—personality, psychology, and politics. Writing a memo to your department head usually requires a different approach than writing a memo to your peers. While writing, keep the *personality* of the reader in mind. Make sure the memo (or letter) accurately reflects your personality. Imagine yourself *saying* the words that you have just put down on paper. Do they sound like you?

Psychology is a critical issue. Answer the following questions about what you wrote. Are you criticizing (or suggesting) something without knowing all the facts? Are you inadvertently taking someone to task? Look at the language of the correspondence—do the words fit the intended message? A suggestion expressed harshly will fail because of the wording, not the idea. Make sure the words suit the idea.

Politics, the last "P," can be the most sensitive. In today's uncertain corporate environment, politics plays a major role in decision making. Is everyone on the circulation list who should be copied? In one case, a newly named senior vice president sent a letter to an outside consultant, retained his services, and failed to notify the director of the department (who reported to her). He never received a copy of the letter, nor was he informed verbally.

The director had spent more than 20 years at the company and had built up a significant number of political connections. He went to one of those connections to complain about the lack of communication. It was not long before the CEO heard about the incident, and the newly named senior vice president was reprimanded by the president. The respect she lost was never recovered.

This chain of events is indicative of what can occur when organizational politics are ignored. Holding on to your outgoing correspondence for a day will give you time to consider any possible political ramifications.

12. Remember brevity. Quality is more important than quantity. Good writing does not have to fill the page. Keep in mind that your main goal is communication.

INGREDIENTS OF *GOOD* LETTERS AND MEMOS

The following list pairs the characteristics of good and poor letters and memos:

Good	_Poor_
Specific	General
Logical	Abstract
Informal	Formal
Succinct	Rambling
Interesting	Dull
Descriptive	Exaggerated
Verbs used frequently	Adjectives used excessively
Active	Indefinite
Organized	Disorganized
Flowing	Nondirectional
Easy to understand	Technical and esoteric
Word usage economical	Word usage excessive
Complete message	Incomplete message
Accurate information	Inaccurate information

Avoid redundancies. What's the difference between "very effective" and "effective"; "advance planning" and "planning"; "general public" and "public"; "ask the question" and "ask"; "brand new" and "new"? The tendency of most writers is to add words, not delete them.

FORMAL VS. INFORMAL

The tone of your correspondence is important. Tone conveys an attitude, emotion, or feeling through formal or informal expression. In speech, tone can be enhanced with body language, gestures, and facial expressions. A word can take on new meaning with the raising of an arm, the shrug of a shoulder, or a movement of the head. In writing, tone is conveyed solely by the language. Compare the following examples.

> Whether or not we replace the generator will require the prompt attention of the supervisor and those within his department. The ultimate decision is up to that division, and it matters little what our group has to say about it.

> Whether we replace the generator or not is up to the division supervisor. Frankly, it doesn't matter what our group thinks.

The first example is formal, the second is informal. Which one are you more comfortable with? The key to selecting the correct tone is being "natural." Letter and memo writers should not become stilted simply because they are writing instead of talking. Natural tone, a tone similar to the way you talk, is the preferred approach in most letters and memos.

Another element of tone is positive versus negative. "We will try" says something very different from "We will."

Letter and memo authors tend to be so wordy that their text is nonsensical, to focus on length instead of on meaning, and to cloud their words and concepts with abstractions. The following memo was written by the head of the English department at a major university:

> The president may award to tenure any individual including one whose appointment and assignment is in an administrative position, at the time of appointment.

The professor meant that the "president can award tenure to anyone, including someone who happens to be serving in an administrative position."

How can the letter/memo writer acquire a clear focus on meaning? One way is to study the advertising industry. Advertising agencies prosper only if their ads are clear, articulate, and communicative.

Advertisements are good examples of effective, attention-getting writing. Letter and memo writers can obtain valuable insight from advertising copy. On the printed page, every line of type takes space and cost money. Ever cognizant of this fact, copywriters make every word count. Thus, a well-put-together ad is a concise story that gets its point across. It communicates a *unique selling proposition* (USP).

THE USP

What is a USP and how does it relate to the letter and memo writer? Each product or service advertised has some characteristic that sets it apart from its competition. If one car has been judged "safest" of all the automobiles on the road, that's the car's USP. The copywriter finds the one element in the product or service that sets it apart from all other similar products.

An engineer, scientist, or professional who is trying to sell the reader of a letter or memo a concept or need must find the USP—something different that impacts the reader. For instance, in the following memo, written to senior management, an engineer was trying to convince the executives that his design for a product (a valve) was better than any other because it had several capabilities that other valves lacked (the valve's USP).

For the past three months, we have been perfecting an approach to valves that will give our vehicles 50,000 more miles than our closest competitor before they need servicing. In the past 30 days, we have perfected the _____ , a unit that will provide us with the added mileage, and it will not cost any more to produce than our present valves.

This memo contains two of the best USPs: higher quality and no increased cost. Another engineer faced a similar problem when trying to convince senior executives of the need for a larger budget (the product). His reasons (the USPs) are excellent examples of how to make a memo stand out from the crowd.

As you know, the Environmental Protection Agency (EPA) has been steadily tightening its regulations relating to all pesticide products that are to be used on animals. Lately, we have seen several states follow suit by refusing to let kennels and other major users of pesticides order and use such products if they have not been licensed.

It is clear that the regulatory rules are tightening. Within the next five years, we expect that at least 50% of all states will have similar legislation. At present, 15 states have proposed restrictive legislation on the floor. A report from our legislative analyst warns of (1) increased taxes by each state on all pesticides and (2) a growing, vocal opposition that will soon prevent our customers from emptying poisons, even though they may be diluted, down wastewater drains.

The message is clear: Within five years we had best be producing a number of nonpesticide products, or we should be hoping that the legislators are slow.

It is unlikely that Congress will slow its pace, especially if the minority party wins this November's election (as is expected). We need to devote more funds to researching and developing nonpoisonous products that will kill pests but will not be a threat to the environment. We have two such prototypes currently under test. They are _____ and _____. The latter has shown remarkable promise; however, it will take another six months of testing to determine whether we have an effective but "safe" killer. From there, it will take two to three years for EPA approval.

Time is pressing and will soon impact our profitability and our future. To complete the initial test phase on this product, we need a budget increase of 12%, or $300,000, for R&D.

If we have the funding, within four years we could be the leader in this field and dominate a market that has not developed any new, *significantly different* products for years.

Aside from regulatory interference, we have another potential adversary—the consumer, who is becoming increasingly cognizant of the environment and the possible effects of poisons.

With the government on one side and a shrinking market on the other, we should seriously consider upping our R&D immediately.

The memo's USPs are: the government will interfere, profits will be down, markets will close, and consumers will not buy. These are strong arguments for increasing the budget (the move that management ultimately made).

Products and USPs may sound as if they are necessary only for proposals or memos to senior managers, but they are present in almost every piece of correspondence. For quality prose, follow these added suggestions:

1. *Use USP whenever you are trying to convince someone of your argument or case.*

2. *Keep sentences short and conversational.* Try to write the way you talk. Although the two are worlds apart, letters and memos sound natural when they emulate speech.

3. *Write to one person, even if you are writing to 100.* Pretend your message is going to one individual, who is seated just across the room.

4. *Do not coin new words or acronyms.* Writing business letters and memos calls for language that most readers will understand.

5. *Use AIDA and IBC* (both are explained in Chapter 2).

INANE PHRASES

Inane phrases are shallow, empty statements that reflect poor word choice. Some of these phrases may show up in our speech, but we should avoid them in our writing. The following columns match inane phrases with possible alternatives.

Inane Phrase	*Alternative*
during that time	while
after very careful consideration	after considering
whether or not	whether (or regardless)

Inane Phrase	*Alternative*
very good	good
brand new	new
subsequent to	after
be cognizant	know
as of this date	now
during that time period	then
make an examination of	examine
this is a subject that	this subject
the fact of the matter	the fact
make inquiry regarding	inquire (or ask)
inoperative	doesn't work

Many of the statements commonly used in letter and memo writing would sound ridiculous if used in conversation. For this reason, they should be left out of our writing. Imagine *saying* the following:

your valued patronage

yours with respect to same

soliciting your indulgence

please find enclosed

please be advised

regret to state that

regarding said order

may we suggest that

per our records

pursuant to our conversation

regarding said order

Simplifying whenever possible, removing redundant phrases, reading the draft of the correspondence aloud, and following the other suggestions in this chapter will put you on your way to effective writing.

The next chapter examines the structure of good letters and memos, and explores the formulas that enable anyone—writer or not—to master the art of writing letters and memos.

Chapter 2

Why Some Letters and Memos Fail

HOW TO GRAB ATTENTION

- How would you like to make $1 million in the next 24 hours?
- Would you like to be independently wealthy?
- Can our new engineering project earn the company 22% gross profit and increase our bonus pool?

Anyone reading those questions would agree that each commands attention. Whether the subject is personal wealth or a company's well-being, the intrigue is there. Contrast those three sentences with the following:

- The red dye we put into various food substances can be harmful.
- Given the current conditions of the country, would you say the chemical industry will grow?
- Based upon our findings, red meat should be cooked thoroughly.

The first group of sentences automatically grabs us. The second group leaves us flat: our *interest* hasn't been aroused. We are intrigued by the propositions posed in the initial trio, but—unless we are involved in the red dye business, work in the chemical industry, or have a particular preference for how meat is served—the last three have minimal appeal.

In the first group, the sentences resemble headlines and lead sentences in mail-order letters. Each sentence appeals to a basic human instinct and therefore attracts our attention. The first two sentences are directed toward our personal situation, and the third offers a possibility of making money, and creating job security for our company and ourselves.

Grabbing readers' attention, however, takes more than a letter or memo that addresses needs. Consider the following:

> I am pleased to announce that Joseph _____ has been named vice president in charge of manufacturing and support activities. Joseph _____ has been in charge of the engineering division since he came to the company three years ago. Since that time Mr. _____ has demonstrated a great capability to not only handle the technology, but to manage the division with care and concern. Thus, we are putting Mr. _____ in charge of the forthcoming reorganization effort that we will begin next week.

Few employees may care who Mr. _____ is, but they *do* care about reorganization, which usually brings downsizing or layoffs. The reorganization is buried in the memo, and many employees may miss that message because they have failed to get beyond the first few sentences. Information on Mr. _____ does not play to any of their needs or hold their attention. For any letter or memo to do its job, the writer must take hold of recipients' interest by opening with a catchy, attention-getting sentence. Readers' needs have to be addressed, but if they are buried in the body of the memo, they may go unnoticed. Make the opening sentence catchy, and everyone will read it. This opener, in a memo from a manufacturing vice president, caught everyone's attention:

> Our jobs are on the line.

The general manager of an aerospace company got immediate attention by beginning a letter to employees with:

> The only way our company is going to survive is by bringing this project in on time. That means . . . .

The first sentence of a letter or memo can catapult your correspondence into the must-read tray, or it can send your letter straight to the trash basket.

The next time you visit a supermarket, notice where the tabloids are located, and read some of the headlines. Usually, they are up front, near the cash registers. The headlines are classic nonsense:

"Two-headed baby born to Midwest woman," or "East Coast mechanic loses 30 pounds by clipping stomach."

Forget whether the stories are true. Study the headlines. They are attention grabbers. The tabloid headline writers know what will stop consumers and get them to read. The same approach is used by most 6 o'clock TV news broadcasts. The first 10 seconds of the program teases listeners with announcements that "how to find the right mate" or "a special study on how infidelity is sweeping the middle class" will be covered in depth later in the program.

Grabbing readers' or viewers' attention is of paramount importance. Sensationalism is not required, but writers of memos and letters should always keep one thought in mind: The opening needs to be a grabber or recipients won't read the entire document. To make it a grabber, put something important in that first sentence—something that focuses on readers' needs.

Beginning a letter or memo is that simple. Communicate something important in your first sentence, and you have a reader. Regardless of the subject—aerospace, high tech, medicine, or science—the opening line is critical.

AIDA: A FOUR-STEP FORMULA

Letter and memo writers are seldom professional or published writers. The key to success, even for a person who finds it difficult to put ideas on paper, is a simple, four-step formula called AIDA:

1. **Attention.**

2. **Interest.**

3. **Desire.**

4. **Action.**

This age-old approach, used by copywriters in the advertising field, is designed to (1) attract attention, (2) generate interest, (3) build desire, and (4) cause action. Satisfy these four steps and your letter or memo will have an impact on your readers every time.

Effective letters are similar to good advertisements written by talented copywriters. They follow the four-step AIDA structure, and they communicate or "sell" the writers' ideas. Even thank-you notes accomplish selling by (1) expressing appreciation and (2) convincing the recipient of the writer's sincerity.

Leaf through this Sunday's newspaper, and note the ads that capture your attention. Almost without exception, they will have a catchy or provocative headline (also called a lead).

Are You Being Poisoned?

That is the lead for a full-page ad that has run for more than three years in pet magazines. It touts an all-natural flea shampoo, and lets readers know that if they are using poisons, pyrethrum, or other harmful chemicals, they could be poisoning themselves as well as their animal.

The Lazy Man's Way to Riches.

One of the most successful direct-response advertisements ever created uses this lead. This full-page ad helped turn its creator into one of the richest mail-order gurus in the country.

How Much Does Joe's Business Make?

This provocative question, used as the headline on a $44 advertisement, helped a struggling entrepreneur turn his initial investment into an enterprise worth nearly $15 million.

Good letters and memos use the same attention-getting process. A comprehensive report is worthless if no one will read it. Some technical writers believe that they are not obligated to draw the readers in and appeal to their needs. They say that their information, on its merits alone, should warrant reading.

Realistically, few people would even consider reading technical material unless their curiosity or self-interest has been roused. Attention-getting opening lines can create that reaction to your correspondence. Your letters and memos won't wind up in the "round file," your thoughts and ideas will come to the attention of your supervisor, and doors of opportunity will have a handle that turns to let you in.

IDENTIFYING WITH RECIPIENTS

If starting with the right lead is so important, how do you develop one? Where do you get the idea? Do you have to spend half a day developing a simple lead sentence? The key to creating an effective lead sentence is to make sure it relates to your readers' needs.

As a reader, how do you react to the following opener?

During the next fiscal year we will be faced with many financial challenges. It will be up to each department to curtail expenditures, and that can be done with individual budgets, submitted to

senior management for approval. With this approach, I believe we
can reduce expenditures by 35% for the following reasons: . . . .

By the second sentence, the reader is bored. Even if the suggestion is feasible, the reader is already gone.

An employee will finish reading a memo written by his or her CEO-employer, but suppose the memo's author is an accountant offering a money-saving suggestion. The memo will get tossed before all of it is read, and valuable information will be missed. Switch the boring opener around and lead off with:

We can reduce our expenditures by 35% during the next fiscal
year, and improve our profitability, if . . . .

The contrast is evident. This lead sentence addresses management's primary concerns—reducing expenditures and improving profitability. A slight revision (addressing the recipient's needs first) gives this proposal a much greater impact.

The next excerpt is from an actual marketing report submitted by an engineer. The engineer had carefully analyzed the company's problems in marketing a new airplane. A two-page synopsis, submitted to the marketing vice president, started this way:

Competition in the commercial airline market is at a 10-year peak.
Airlines are having a difficult time purchasing new equipment because of cash-flow problems, which were exacerbated by an air-
fare war during the first six months of this year. It is expected that
this intense competition will continue for at least another 18
months. During that time, the marketing of the _____ will
be difficult. However, there are ways to ameliorate the situation.
For instance, ...

Communication would have been much simpler—and the memo and suggestion would have gone much further—if the engineer had begun with:

Sales of the _____ can be increased by 15% this year if
we . . . .

Notice the difference. The recipient's interests and needs lie in increasing the sales of the airplane. To grab attention, the memo should address ways of meeting those needs first, rather than discussing market conditions. The opening lines usually determine how well read a letter or memo will be or whether it will be read at all. Call the opening a "hook" or a grabber; whatever you name it, it should intrigue your readers and get them to go on.

Three attention-getting devices that work almost every time are listed here, with examples:

1. Pose questions. They arouse curiosity and encourage the reader to go on.
   — "Would you like to buy your next home with no money down?"
   — "Do you know why the aircraft has failed to sell?"
   — "What would happen if we went to a third shift?"

2. Make bold, brash statements. Outrageous statements stop the reader.
   — "Without increased budget, this project will fail."
   — "We can increase our sales by 15% with one slight change . . . ."
   — "Now is the time for us to change our manufacturing process."

3. Challenge the reader to do something or to stretch toward a high standard.
   — "By approving the following plan, our department will be fully empowered."
   — "Unless this program is underway within 30 days, we will not be able to finish . . . ."
   — "We need your permission for a total reorganization, or the _____ proposal will run _____ days late."

Letter or memo writing becomes easier when you put yourself in the place of the recipients. What are their concerns? What would intrigue them? What would keep their attention? Answer the five questions below *before* you start to compose an attention-getter.

1. What do the recipients need?

2. What are their primary concerns?

3. What are their goals?

4. What are their financial concerns?

5. What problems are pressing or relevant to them.

You don't have to be a Hemingway to find a good attention-getting device. The following opening was written by an engineer who discovered he had made a mistake when giving instructions to a subcontractor.

I blew it. Our materials department apparently made a mistake in giving you the dimensions of the . . . .

Three little words. Few attention-getters can top "I blew it." Another point: your correspondence should not be poetic, wordy, or known for its great number of adjectives. Simple language works best. Remember, people understand simple terms, but you cannot count on their comprehending technical jargon. Keep in mind that the final step of the four-step AIDA formula is "action." Your opening sentence should feature a prominent, active verb.

A physicist opened a letter to a colleague this way:

I'd like to ask you a favor. Next month, one of my dearest friends will be coming into town to evaluate our latest . . . .

The direct approach gets the reader's attention. In the next opening, a scientist was querying the editor of a technical journal about the possibility of reprinting an article in a local newsletter.

I thoroughly enjoyed reading the article on the growth of the Internet and its possible impact on our profession in your *Journal* last month, and I know the members of our local association would be thrilled if they had the opportunity to read the article. Could we have your permission to reprint it in . . . ?

The compliment in the first sentence gets attention, and the reader is eased into the second sentence, where the request is made.

Direct-mail copywriters are masters of attention-getting. Although most of their products are radically different from those of the typical engineer or scientist, their openings can usually be adapted.

"Would you mind if we filled your mailbox with money?"

This guaranteed attention-getter could be adapted by any professional to read:

"Would you mind if our fourth quarter was the most profitable in our history?

"Would you mind if we were able to trim our expenditures by 25%?"

"Would you mind if our aerospace company was 15% ahead of our nearest competitor?"

FACTS AND TRUTH: THEIR IMPACT

Regardless of the verbiage used in the opening, the words are not there merely to attract attention. They should be factual and truthful. Never write a misleading lead. A dynamic attention-getter is fraudulent if it leads the reader on, and then the rest of the letter or memo has nothing to do with the lead. If clever words are used to attract attention but have nothing to do with the content of the letter, the writer loses credibility—and readers. Gimmick leads are quickly routed to the round file, and they usually stir up resentment for wasting the recipients' time.

"You can cut 25% off your production costs."

That kind of attention-getting lead had better have a payoff. If it is a statement made by a company's manufacturing vice president, readers will take notice. But if it is the opening sentence of a computerized sales letter from a telephone company, it will be trashed. Recipients recognize the differences (and the needs) immediately.

"With one change in your manufacturing process, you could become the leader in your industry. . . ."

This big, bold, promising attention-getter came from a temporary help agency that was trying to persuade the manufacturer to replace permanent employees with those on contract. Hiring outsiders versus insiders does not translate to becoming an industry leader. But suppose the line had read:

"There is a way for your company to improve its performance and profitability—but change is involved."

This version is intriguing because it does not promise the moon. The original letter went on to explain (with supporting numbers) how outside labor has saved some companies enormous sums of money. No claim was made for this specific firm, but the letter proposed a no-cost assessment for the firm—an attention-getting and realistic device.

Another opening used a catchy lead, but was not misleading:

We don't promise, we deliver. Other courier services promise you the moon, and usually they deliver—late. We don't promise anything but on-time, rapid service. In 20 years, _____ has never failed to . . . .

This opening was written by a supplier to a chemical manufacturer:

"How reliable is the sodium lauryl sulfate you are using? Have you checked the efficacy lately?"

CREATING INTEREST

Good openings stimulate the reader to find out more about the subject being addressed. The catchy first (or second) sentence should take the reader to the next element of the AIDA formula—interest. A note that has become a classic because of its attention-getting opening and its follow-up interest goes as follows:

> (opening attention getter) Did Ponce de Leon really discover a fountain of youth in Florida or did he merely have a great public relations man?

> (interest) We will probably never know the answer. So many questions like this one still remain because they have come about through word-of-mouth and not historical fact. Word-of-mouth has, more than anything else, the power to create legends . . . .

The interest portion of the letter does not totally divorce itself from the opening. It does not abandon the Ponce de Leon query and leave readers with the feeling they have been had. Interest amplifies and expands the opening statement. It carries readers from the first sentence through a *fact-filled* section—usually the body of the letter or memo. Interest contains facts.

Notice the technique utilized in the following memo. An engineer is notifying management about a problem element in the production line:

> The _____ are on the verge of collapse. The prime problem is in the _____ itself, which skips every other coupling and causes hours of delay because we have to stop the line and go back to the missed couplings. In addition to stopping the line, we also have to make . . . .

After an attention-getting opening, the second sentence follows logically. Most attention-getters run only a sentence or two. The interest section, however, may need three or more paragraphs.

> (attention) Our new _____ units are difficult to market because they are priced 10% higher than our competitor's models. (interest) The higher price is due to several factors, such as the labor costs we have involved in our line versus _____ .

Another factor adding to the cost is shipping. Our units weigh nearly 25% more than others in the industry, and our finishing plant is on the West Coast. This leaves us with a heavier product and a longer distance.

The higher price will be of interest to management, and the pricing statement is limited to one sentence. The interest begins with the second sentence and continues to the end of the paragraph. Following this rationale, the interest section could contain several paragraphs, each giving additional reasons for the higher price.

(attention) The necessity for our presence on the World Wide Web is based upon misinformation and an increasing amount of hyperbole that is sweeping across our industry. (interest) In examining our competitor's positions, I found that only two other electronic firms had any significant presence on the Web. A number of subcontractor films were located there, but after spending several hours on the telephone with three of them, it became apparent that none was sure of the results, if any. Our customers' questions as to where we are on the Web are apparently being asked out of curiosity. I had a lengthy discussion with _____ Industries, and they showed little concern when I told them we were not on the Web, nor did we have immediate plans of getting on it.

A strong opening attracts the reader, and the interest section provides backup to the opening. Here are some examples.

(attention) To decide which facility should be closed, we should concern ourselves with two primary issues—cost savings and people cost. (interest) When it comes to evaluating the former, it is clear that closing the _____ plant makes the most sense because its costs are nearly 40% higher than our _____ facility. But, regarding people cost, we have a dilemma. Both the _____ and _____ facilities are running up high productivity costs when compared to our other plants, but both facilities are the backbone employer of two depressed areas. Closing either one would hurt the region economically and would give _____ Industries, Inc. a bad name.

(attention) Eliminating our graveyard shift would save us 21% of our payroll costs, but would cost us 35% of our production. (interest) In examining the production and labor records, one fact about the graveyard crew becomes clear. Although they cost us a premium wage, they produce more than any comparable crew. This increased productivity may be the result of quieter work areas and less distractions, or . . . .

(attention) The race for the first antigen to be produced by a _____ laboratory is over, and the winner of the competition is _____ . (interest) This battle between our company and _____ and _____ has been going on for more than four years, and in winning it we have learned several things. Initially, we rushed into experimentation and had numerous scientific crews . . . .

CREATING DESIRE

Attention and interest lead the reader to the third step in the AIDA formula—creating desire on the part of the recipient to do something. The attention-getter is short and to the point—perhaps one sentence, designed to appeal to the reader's curiosity. Interest, the back-up for attention, offers proofs, facts, and validating statements. This combination leads to desire, which is a transition between interest and action. Desire to do something builds within the reader, and a willingness to take action (do something) develops because benefits are built into the desire section. Desire relates to the recipient and their interests.

(attention) Our project needs immediate overhaul or we will not be able to complete it on time. (interest) Apparently, the _____ . lens, which we had designed, is not calculating our formula correctly. Aside from the obvious mistakes in the process, we have to repeat the procedure. At the end of the loop, when the finished _____ . are ready, we cannot be sure that the diameter is the right thickness, because of the potential formula miscalculations. (desire) Needless to say, this problem has put our project goals at least 30 days behind schedule and will impact your department and its delivery schedule. If we can get to the bottom of the problem and solve our difficulties, the solution will not only be beneficial to me and the company, but will also impact your area's performance. If we do not handle the problem immediately, I foresee your area falling even further behind than ours is right now.

Notice how urgency is being created in the recipient's mind. The writer stresses that the recipient's goals, as well as his own, will be skewed. That message makes this memo effective. There is an urgent need to do something, and the desire for action is prodded by information on what will happen if something is not accomplished quickly.

(attention) We've just finished our investigation into the booster's failure, and we've uncovered some definite flaws that will help your area in future designs.

(interest) First, the diameter of the _____ engine is _____. After several additional experiments in the _____ , we discovered that this does not leave enough room for the _____. Alloys are being used that we are not sure about. Initial tests on the metals were fine, but the calibration does not register anywhere near what it should be.

(desire) Continued usage of the booster endangers the _____ of the _____ group and reflects on our unit's integrity. I know we've discussed your department's quality control, which is among the best in the industry. However, if we continue to generate the same response from clients that we have received during the past few months, the amount of business we will be doing in the future is questionable. Our current backlog has shrunk to 30 days, the lowest we have had in almost 2 years. If we go beneath 2 weeks, we will have to look at the feasibility of either short-term layoffs or reduced hours for some of the nonexempt employees.

The following memo was from a supervisor to his staff.

(attention) Effective communication is always a problem—especially when it comes to technical data—and our department is no exception.

(interest) Each of us is busy at work on our own projects and problems. We seldom take time to see what our colleagues are doing or how it can impact our area. (desire) After six months of running our department, I see a need for change. I hope all of you share my view. We have many issues that we should be discussing as a group. With that approach, I believe our workload would be easier, and the interaction in our department would increase to where each of us would be more efficient—and not work as hard.

The supervisor is setting the stage for action. Because everyone would like to have an easier workload, it is relatively easy to build desire. The benefits (to the reader) become prominent in the desire section.

Desire is also created in this letter to an external vendor.

(attention) When we awarded the _____ , we envisioned that our timetable would allow us to give your company until the end of the year for the initial designs. However, our situation has been changing rapidly.

(interest) As you may know, a tender offer has been made for our company's stock. Usually, that fact would remain in the domain of our board of directors, but because of the nature of the buyer, it may impact us. (desire) The _____ Company is quite proficient at design, and I believe if the offer is accepted by our board it could affect the way we do business as well as our relationship with all our subcontractors. The entire project could conceivably be outsourced to a firm that is capable of handling all its components. If this step is taken, the impact would be felt by our internal workforce, your firm, and every subcontractor working for us. Yesterday, in a conversation with Mr. _____ of your firm, I communicated the present urgency. Mr. _____ had several suggestions on how my company and your company could expedite the present plans before any merger problems become reality.

The desire builds because of the facts. The subcontractor could lose business, but the writer of the letter may have a solution. This possibility will lead into the action portion of the letter.

In the following letter, a journal article authored by an engineer is being requested for reprinting:

(attention) I just finished reading your article on "Mass Transit in the Cities: Engineering Myth or Potential Boom," and found it to be extremely informative as well as a fascinating report on the difficulties of engineering mass transit routes. (interest) Some of the points you make about route selection and automotive versus transit system travel were eye-openers. Your discussion covering whether we could ever truly get drivers out of their cars especially caught my interest. There may be ways.

(desire) Our organization circulates a monthly newsletter to more than 25,000 subscribers. Our members would be greatly interested in transit travel's psychological and physical barriers. In several upcoming issues, there will be a "bonus" circulation: we have made special arrangements with Comdex to provide an extra

100,000 copies. Your article in one of these issues would both enhance the publication and put you in touch with thousands of people who are in a position to utilize your services.

Imagine the next paragraph (action), which would tie the entire letter together.

(action) If you would give us permission to reprint your article, we could reach those members and make them aware of your availability.

Here are some additional letters and memos that illustrate the AID format:

(attention) The silicon chip that we developed as the basis for the _____ has developed some problems. (interest) Although we have not received any complaints from vendors, our in-house test units, which are older and have been under test conditions much longer than anything we have on the market, have started to develop a coating that is causing data to be lost. The disturbing thing about the coating is that the older the unit gets, the faster the coating accumulates.

(desire) Although none of our internal sales or marketing staff know of the problem, we are going to have to take action soon, to make them aware of potential customer complaints. We have managed to solve some of the coating problem by substituting a _____ and discarding the chip. This same procedure could work with the units we have in the field, but the number grows each day, making the problem more difficult to manage. We have explored several alternatives and feel that with the right plan we might be able to remedy our field problems and satisfy our customers.

———————

(attention) We have problems with our new batches of cleaning products, especially those that carry _____ as the prime cleanser.

(interest) Initially, we had a few scattered customer complaints. They focused primarily on the cleanser's being difficult to rinse, which is a problem we have never had. Other clients said the cleanser was not cleaning as thoroughly, and still others called to say the cleanser was beginning to leave a film over whatever it was used on.

(desire) In tracking our repeat sales orders from these groups, we found that our reorders had dropped nearly 40%. The _____ Company, with its _____ cleanser, had picked up nearly half of our repeat business. This trend is disturbing and does not bode well for our division. We need a plan of action, and it must be put together quickly.

——————————

(attention) Do you want to make an additional 15% profit from your engineering group? (interest) The _____ Company and the _____ Corporation have been able to increase their profits more than 12% with our simple technique. (desire) All it takes is approximately one hour of your time. We can show you, at no cost, how to escalate your profitability. This is not a gimmick. In fact, we guarantee the results, and if you do not think we are giving you the best advice possible, tell us and we will leave at any time during the presentation.

The following letter, from an athletic booster to an outstanding college prospect, is an example of how broad-based AIDA can be. It works for communications that run the gamut from high-tech production to professional athletics.

(attention) You have the potential to become one of the finest professional athletes this country has ever seen. (interest) Your quickness, strength, and dedication are characteristics that I have seen in very few people. It is obvious that you train hard, long hours and that your work ethic is topped only by your loyalty.

(desire) You can easily turn those characteristics into attributes that will help you get into college and build for your future. With a few simple changes, your playing ability and accomplishments can be twice as effective.

HOW TO GENERATE ACTION

The letters and memos that follow are excellent examples of how attention, interest, and desire can lead to action.

(attention) I sent this letter several weeks ago, but it is so important I decided to resend it.

(interest) As an interested member of our community, I know you have been involved in as many charitable endeavors as I have—the

YMCA fund-raiser, the Habitat for Humanity drive, and so many others. We have both been there—together.

(desire) We have an opportunity to tackle a project that will do more good than anything we have ever worked on. The project involved will take no more than two or three evenings during the next four months. Yet, what we can accomplish in those two or three evenings will mean more to a certain segment of our population than winning the lottery.

What is it? What's the payoff? What does the reader have to do? The letter was soliciting local citizens to donate time to help raise funds for a new community center. The letter has all the elements that intrigue readers, getting them ready for the desire portion of the letter. The following letter achieves the same purpose.

(attention) As a new mother, there are moments you will never forget. (interest) The first cry of your baby. The day you both came home. The look of delight on your husband's face when he saw your child for the first time.

(desire) All those moments were captured, or were they? Like most parents, you probably have a camera—perhaps even a camcorder. But did you know that there are other, better ways to capture those moments? There are techniques that make camcorders and still pictures look obsolete. These techniques are revolutionary *and* affordable. They will give you countless moments of joy today, tomorrow, and years from now, when your youngster is grown and giving you grandchildren.

The next letter is short but contains some powerful words in the opening (attention) segment. These words are usually associated with poetry and nontechnical industries. The writer showed that the same vocabulary could be equally effective in a highly scientific field.

(attention) You are going to love this proposal. (interest) The chemists in the bio lab have been running out of _____ materials for the DNA experiments, and they had a (desire) suggestion that might solve the problem and be more productive at the same time. Their idea would also enable our company to reduce product costs.

The letter below was sent by a computer consultant to a prospective small business client. It could have been keyboarded by any professional, with the service and/or product slightly altered.

(attention) If your business is not where you would like it to be, perhaps you are not using the correct marketing techniques. (interest) Have you been able to generate any new clients this month? Or, is the number of your new clients below your goal? Are you losing clients, and wondering why? Are you having difficulty keeping track of clients?

(desire) I offer techniques that you can utilize to remedy any of these situations. My techniques can help you build your business without spending any more on marketing than you have currently budgeted. . . .

Another example originated in the aerospace industry.

(attention) Is our enterprise about to be shut down? Are we going to be another company that is listed as a victim of the cutbacks in aerospace?

(interest) In the past two years, almost half of our competitors have either gone out of business or merged with other firms. The pot is getting smaller: the dollar amount that Congress has appropriated for R&D has been cut in half during the past 36 months. Our company depends on those R&D moneys, and last month we saw a further cut in the budget.

(desire) There are things we can do about it. There are programs we can initiate that will show Congress we are interested in making aerospace an industry of the future as well as the past.

The next example, an internal memo written by the CEO of a major aerospace company, got every employee's attention. It was an excellent lead-in to the action that the president desired.

(attention) I want all department managers to begin to think of their areas as small businesses or their own small business. (interest) Think about the telephone, lights, stationery—even the paper clips. Think about how you would watch and preserve them if you were running your own business. (desire) If we begin to think of our departments as our own businesses, we'll find ways to make those departments not only more cost-conscious, but more profitable as well. That's what we need. In today's aerospace industry, without your input, your efforts, and your teamwork, our company is not going to be around. But with your help, our firm will not only stay around but will thrive and prosper. (action) So when you turn the lights on tomorrow morning, remember one thing: This is not the business of _____ Industries, it is *your* business.

The first three parts of the AIDA formula set the stage for action—something the recipient can *do*. The following letter, sent to a colleague by a professional seeking advice and an alliance, illustrates all four AIDA steps.

> (attention) Your reputation as an incredible speaker with extraordinary knowledge about _____ has everyone in our organization talking. (interest) As you may know, _____ is something our entire group has spent a good deal of time analyzing. To date, we've submitted a half-dozen papers to the _____ *Journal* and have had excellent reaction to our theories. Listening to the tape that _____ sent us from your talk, we realized how much additional material has been developed on _____ in the past two years. Your thoughts as to how the _____ replicates, and what it will mean to our _____ projects in the future, enabled us to see how your theories coincide with those we have developed.
>
> (desire) The knowledge you have would be extraordinarily beneficial to our group. It could not only help us, but I think our success with various processes could stimulate some ideas for you, too.
>
> (action) A joint meeting between your engineering group and ours would be quite beneficial. We have just uncovered several new aspects to the _____ .

A desire for action is developed in the recipient through recognition of the benefits to both parties. The engineer receiving the above letter sees that a meeting could be extremely helpful to his own cause if he is willing to share his information and to listen to some colleagues.

After a writer has developed a strong enough desire within the recipient, it is time to introduce the action that should take place. Desire brings the recipient to the point of taking action. Here are some other examples of the four AIDA steps and how they can be structured in letters and memos.

> (attention) I need your help and advice.
>
> (interest) Our department is considering the installation of a _____ system; however, there are certain parameters it must fulfill. We have not had the opportunity to see the system in operation, but I understand you have been working with it for the past year.

(desire) Your assistance in answering a few questions would enable us to evaluate the system and could save us countless hours of research—and dollars. If you could answer the following, I'll owe you—at least one!

(action) How long have you had the system? How much down time have you had with it?
Has it enabled you to cut overhead? If so, to what extent?
Would you recommend the system? Would you consider it for our department? If not, why?
Are there any other systems you would recommend?

(attention) I hope your sabbatical rested you sufficiently. Now that you're back, we need your help!

(interest) While you were gone, we were given one of the most difficult projects in the company. You know what it is: the development of the _____ plan and program. The problem we encounter most is that the technology involved changes rapidly. When we formulated the first phase of the plan, we were planning to use _____ , but by the time we were ready it was outdated.

(desire) That's one of the reasons why we are glad to see you return. Before you left, you were working on an intriguing addendum to strategic plans, which enabled each department to project technology innovation along with the plan's progress. It was a fascinating approach and now we would like to take advantage of it.

(action) During the next week, our group will be meeting in an attempt to forecast the technology that will impact the project. If you could join us and assist us in gauging our present technology against future innovations, it would be extremely helpful. The session has been set for Monday, November 10, at 9 A.M., in the main conference room. Please let us know whether you will be able to join us for the session.

IBC: ANOTHER WINNING FORMULA

Although AIDA is a relatively simple formula, it is not the only approach to letter and memo writing. An equally effective and even easier method is called Introduction, Body, and Conclusion (IBC). Speakers have used it for years. If you ever took a college speech course, you may have encountered it there. Numerous English teachers still preach the sequence when instructing their students how to write short stories, reports, and speeches. By following IBC, you can prepare memos and letters just as you would a speech. In many ways, the two kinds of products are exactly alike. Good speeches communicate, and so do good memos or letters.

IBC can also be used for presentations, reports, journal articles, and proposals.

Although the IBC concept is familiar, how to approach it may be a puzzle. Typically, when using the IBC format, the writer concentrates first on an effective opening, just as we did earlier when learning the attention step of AIDA. An introduction, like an attention-getter, is usually not long—perhaps a sentence or two. The body (similar to AIDA's interest and desire sections) forms the bulk of the document. The conclusion, the last element, is usually no longer than the introduction (or attention-getter).

CONCLUSION: A KEY TO BEGINNING

Here's an approach—or gimmick—that will make the IBC approach one of the most effective tools in your writing workshop. Instead of crafting the Introduction first, think about the conclusion and make some decisions:

How do you want the letter to end?

What point do you want to make?

What message do you want to communicate?

What action are you going to propose?

Answers to those questions will create your conclusion. Before thinking of an introduction or filling in the body, structure your conclusion by answering those questions. The conclusion should have tremendous impact for your readers. To ensure that level of impact, do what many speechwriters do: they work on the ending first, and then write a speech that logically leads to the finished ending. They ask themselves: "What conclusion do I want to make? What message do I want to convey? What action do I want my audience to take?"

Memo and letter writers can adopt the same approach. By dwelling on the conclusion initially, memo and letter writers can avoid writers' number-one mistake: writing before they think. When that mistake is made, the written piece rambles.

Engineers, scientists, and other professionals have a clear idea of the information they want to convey, but that clarity gets blurred when they begin writing before they know what their conclusion will say. Without listing the points they will make in the conclusion, even the best memo and letter writers may find themselves wasting paper.

Find your conclusion, then backpedal to the opening. Ask yourself: "What should my conclusion be? What do I want it to be? Am I going to end by asking a question? Am I proposing a solution or decision? What will it be?"

Suppose a department head wants to hire another worker to enable production to increase by 25%. The conclusion is: If we hire another worker, we can increase sales by 25%.

The next step is to fill in the body and the introduction ("How would you like to increase sales by 25% and spend only a fraction of that amount in order to do so?") The relationship between your introduction and conclusion should be strong and clear. These sections tie together and may even have similar wording.

With this approach, the body would contain proofs, facts, figures, costs, and other data on what would be involved if someone new were hired. The body would back up the two other aspects of the document.

The body is usually the longest part of the memo because it contains all the proofs, evidence, facts, and related information. Usually, the opening (introduction) is no longer than the conclusion.

Here is a conclusion in a memo pertaining to an assembly line:

Let's move the radio placement 2 inches to the left on the dashboard, so we can save assembly time and cut a minimum of 30 minutes off the production of each model.

The introduction would be derived from the conclusion:

We can cut a minimum of 30 minutes off the fabrication of each model, if we move the radio placement 2 inches to the left on the dashboard.

The sentence almost duplicates the conclusion. The body would contain all the proof needed to back up the claim.

IBC works in every situation.

(conclusion) Our strategic planning meeting should be scheduled for September 1, if each department is going to get its 1997 plans prepared on time.

(introduction) If our departments are going to get their 1997 plans prepared on time, we must hold the Strategic Planning Meeting no later than September 1.

In another example, only the sentence structure is varied:

(conclusion) The mutation in the DNA is not the cause of the abnormality.

(introduction) One question has puzzled all of us: Is the DNA mutation the cause of the abnormality?

Between the introduction and the conclusion, readers would find the body—the evidence that supports the conclusion.

The body, incidentally, does not have to be peppered with colorful language or hype. If you examine most speeches, the introduction and conclusion deliver the real one-two punch. Although not bereft of all flair and style, the Body serves up primarily factual information. Any conscientious information gatherer can put it together. Someone who can organize facts and data to support an argument or theory can produce a readable body without serious problems.

AIDA and IBC are examples of the many simple techniques that you can use to write more readable letters and memos. Many published authors are not naturally good communicators. They just learned which writing formulas worked best for them.

Chapter 3

The Eleven Most Common Letter Mistakes— How to Avoid Them

It is a sobering thought that each of us gives his hearers and his readers a chance to look into the inner workings of his mind when he speaks or writes.

J. M. Baker

1. TYPOS

The engineering consultant had worked on the proposal for weeks. It was his chance to land the one account that would solidify his business. He had toured the client's facilities on several occasions, talked to everyone from the guard at the gate to the president of the firm, and he was ready. He took one more look at the proposal. He hadn't missed anything.

That afternoon, he personally delivered the document to the president's office. There were additional copies for the vice president of manufacturing, the design engineer's office, and the chief financial officer. Afterward, he began calculating how long it would be before he heard from the prospect. The proposal was not complex, and the consultant was sure the executives would be able to read it, compare notes, and get back to him within two weeks.

When the telephone rang that afternoon, he was both delighted and shocked. It was the president's secretary, thanking him for the proposal, and saying that although the chief executive—and the others—appreciated the work that went into it, they were going to "pass for now." They had thought it over and decided it was premature to be hiring anyone.

Shocked, the consultant wondered what happened. Why had they suddenly changed their goals? Was it something he did, or something he had failed to do?

Nearly two years went by before the consultant discovered what had happened. When he heard the reason, he could hardly believe it, but it turned out to be true. Although the CEO and other executives liked the consultant, the president had certain "quirks." When the proposal was delivered to him, the first page—where his name and title were neatly typed—disturbed him and kept him from reading any further. There, in the middle of the page, was his full title and name:

Presidnent Alan Jacobs

As silly as it may sound, typographical errors are the most common mistakes made in letters. Recipients' reactions vary from indifferent to insulted. Alan Jacobs' reaction was that he had been insulted. He thought, "If this consultant does not care enough or is not careful enough to spell my title correctly, then perhaps he does not care enough to make sure his recommendations are correct." Typos show the reader that the writer is careless and inaccurate. If you make spelling mistakes, then—in the recipient's mind—the information and suggestions you are presenting in your letters could also be mistakes. Here's an example of a simple thank-you note ruined by a typo.

Dear _____

Thanks for the time you took to meat with John and me. You can be sure our proposal will give you a great deal to think about. We look forward to seeing you in the near future.

Newspaper editors receive hundreds of news releases each day, and when deciding which stories are worthwhile, many go by the rule that if the document is mispelled, it must not be important.

Most computer software programs on the market today have a spell check or other similar device, but these devices can only check for spelling errors; they cannot tell you if you have used the wrong word. Double-check all correspondence yourself. Do not rely on a spell check program or a secretary to make sure your written communications are correct. If you write the letter or memo yourself, hold it overnight and check it the next morning.

2. TECHNICAL TERMS

More often than not, correspondence written by an engineer will be read by nonengineers. A letter full of technical terminology will lose its meaning for readers not knowledgeable in the professional lingo.

Engineers, scientists, and other professionals should always keep in mind the level of technical knowledge of their correspondence readers. Write on a level that anyone within your company can understand. Do not use jargon and acronyms. If you cannot exclude the jargon and acronyms, include an "executive summary." The summary should be a recap, usually one or two paragraphs, that enables anyone to get the gist of the letter or memo without reading through the entire document.

For instance, suppose a letter is written by a scientific department seeking funds for a new project. All the scientists within the department, and the department head, read the document, agree with it, and endorse the project.

The correspondence works its way up through the company, and eventually the chief financial officer (CFO) reads it. Within ten minutes the CFO rejects the request for funds. Let's look at the letter to see why this request would be turned down so quickly.

> The RFK-1 _____ is of critical importance to this department. Without it, we will not be able to conduct CASN studies, nor will we be able to determine the ALV levels of the _____ product line. Therefore, without delay, I would like to request _____ dollars to purchase the unit as soon as possible.

The letter breaks a basic rule of letter writing—it is not written for the "lowest common denominator." The letter was designed to generate funding for a project, and should have been written in language that the chief financial officer would understand.

3. THE LOWEST COMMON DENOMINATOR

Remember, the challenge in letter or memo writing is to write for the lowest common denominator. Write in language that anyone who might receive your correspondence (not just someone with your professional specialty) can understand. Newspapers, for instance, are written in language and structure that 8th graders can understand. In newspapers, the 8th grader is the lowest common denominator.

4. NEEDS RECOGNITION

When a person walks into an automobile dealership, the first thing a good salesperson determines is "What kind of car does this person need and why?" The salesperson tries to ascertain the needs of the buyer in order to satisfy those needs.

Buying an automobile and writing a letter proposing a new product may seem worlds apart, but each has a buyer (the car buyer and the letter recipient) and each of those buyers has needs. In other words, if I am sending a request to my manager for new software (my need), I should be cognizant of his or her needs, too. The manager's needs may revolve around budget. Perhaps no funds are available for the software, and my request is turned down because of the money involved. The following letter was sent to a supervisor by one of his departmental employees.

> As you know, we have required the _____ software to add to our _____ program for the past four months. This will make our jobs much easier, and enable us to do things that we have not been able to do to this point. The cost of the software is $_____ , which may not be included in our expenditures this fiscal year, but appropriating funds for it would be of great benefit to our department.

This letter does not address needs; it addresses wants. The supervisor sent the letter back to the employee, and asked for a letter that would justify the expenditure. With the help of several other people in the department, the letter was revised.

> Our _____ project is running behind and taking us approximately twice the normal time to complete because we have a software problem. Instead of the _____ , we should purchase the _____ , a software system that will enable us to check our calculations in one-half the time. Presently, we spend 28% more in overtime because the _____ software is slow, and we need to put people on extra shifts in order to compensate for the delay. If we expended the $_____ for the new software, we would make up for the dollars within two months by not having to pay overtime. This would not only enable us to produce the unit faster, but it would make our product more cost effective. Even though we do not have the monies allocated, if we do not purchase the software we will end the fiscal year more than $25,000 in the red because of overtime. If we buy the software, we will not only

come in below the $25,000 figure, but we will come in below budget thanks to the speed and efficiency of the software.

The original correspondence gave the supervisor no reason to approve the request. There was no validation of the employee's argument that the old software was costing the company money. In the revised correspondence, the employee cites figures and he explains how the software will benefit the entire department.

Keep the following needs in mind when making a request.

- My needs revolve around the improvement this request would bring about.

- My manager's needs involve the company, profits, and increasing productivity.

The most effective correspondence you can write will (a) address your needs, (b) address the manager's needs, (c) show how the request will impact the company, and (d) show how the request is worth the expenditure.

When writing a letter that involves expending funds or changing a process, always remember the impact the correspondence might have on the people responsible for approving the expenditure. No one likes change; but if that change has benefits, acceptance of it is more likely.

5. OBJECTIVITY

Passion may be fine for politicians who are trying to arouse their constituents, but at the business level, passionate language does not help sell. Businesspeople want to make decisions on an objective level. They want the facts presented, so that they can make a decision based on those facts.

Colorful, upbeat language can be used in a letter, provided that the writer has objective backup for any claims and statements presented. A lack of objectivity destroys the writer's credibility and renders the letter ineffective.

It has come to my attention that Group B was selected to lead the research and development into the _____ bomber project, and I cannot express too strongly how disturbing that choice is to our people.

If you remember, we were the group that pioneered the proposal and came up with most of the rationale that helped us win the contract in the first place. We were also the group that led our company's research and development into the _____ and _____ , two of the most successful commercial aircraft designs we have ever produced.

To be bypassed for a beginning group that does not have half the experience or credentials that our organization has disturbed all of us.

As project leader, I would like to know why we were ignored after our sterling record.

Complaining loudly does little good, unless the complaints are presented with some objectivity. The reasons why senior management ignored this group could be numerous, but the tone of this letter could prevent the designer and his group from ever getting an answer. The proper way to have addressed this issue would have been to (a) phrase some questions, (b) remind the senior managers of the past accomplishments of the group, and (c) ask what the possibilities might be for readdressing the issue. Examine the revised letter and notice why it does a better job of selling.

Our group was recently made aware that another section was chosen to spearhead the R&D on the _____ bomber project. While we realize that Group B is certainly capable, I've had a number of those within the group asking questions about the decision.

First, were specific criteria set down for the selection? If so, could you let us know what they were and how we differed in performance evaluation from Group B? Knowledge of this will help us in future projects.

Were there extremely important subject areas that management thought were lacking in our group when measured against Group B? Has Group B been trained in specific research and development techniques, relating to the _____ bomber, that we have not handled?

Is management aware that our group pioneered the research and development of both the _____ and _____ , two of the most successful aircraft in our company's history? Is management aware that we will soon be winding down our _____ project, which will free our design engineers for more intense work such as this project?

In the revised correspondence, the project manager is upset about the selection of another contractor, but does not voice any animosity. The project manager poses good questions—questions that will make management think, and questions that will bring to mind the accomplishments of this group. The revised correspondence leaves the door open for management to assign the group to another project.

6. COMPETITION

A letter trying to build yourself up by putting down the competition will be poorly received by the people you are trying to impress.

The letter recipients want to hear what's good about your suggestion or product. They are interested in hearing information about the competition, but they are not interested in hearing the competition belittled in order to make your suggestion or product look better. Showing how your suggestion or product compares to those of a competitive company is permissible, but stay away from opposition bashing. Here's a letter that points out the faults of the competition rather than emphasizing the benefits within the writer's own company.

> We understand our company is being considered along with _____ as prime subcontractors for the _____ . As you know, our firm has been put in similar spots many times, and we perform well. Although I do not believe in knocking competitors, I think it would behoove you to check the references of XXXX Company. I know they have had problems delivering on time, and with the _____ Industries first booster, they ran more than two months behind. Part of the reason is that they do not have the engineering capability of our firm, nor the experience.

This letter is a negative way of approaching a competitive situation. When faced with intense competition, vendors and others vying for contracts should play up their own positives.

One technique to get the edge on competitors without ever saying anything bad about them is to determine where your abilities exceed those of your competitors. The area of excellence should be one that is necessary for the quality production of the product. If your finishing of the product is superior, then play up that capability. Cite statistics, references, and accomplishments in the area of finishing. Emphasizing your area of excellence will cause the letter recipients to make their own comparisons with the competitors' ability in this area. Directing your readers to a point of comparison where the competitors do not measure up can give you the edge. By playing up a strength, you can call attention to a competitor's weakness without putting the competitor down.

7. ORGANIZATION

The average businessperson has little reading time. Thus, business letters should be well-organized and easy-to-read. Look at the pitfalls in the following letter.

> Overtime is required because we need to finish the _____ project by March 1. Right now, we are working an extra shift, but we feel we may have to add another if deadlines are to be met. Still, there are ways we may be able to avoid overtime and bring the project in on time. Frank _____ company has been working simultaneously on the same project, and from all reports we hear they are slightly ahead of us. The monies it would take to catch up to _____ would not warrant the expenditure. Although the rewards will be great when the project is completed, they are hard to ascertain presently. If we were able to work jointly with _____ , we could easily up our timetable, eliminate our overtime, and bring a profitable project into the company. What are your thoughts?

The writer of this letter never gets to the point, and it does not take long for the reader to get confused. Is the writer asking for more overtime? Or less overtime, and help from another company?

The letter rambles, damaging its readability and credibility. The letter lacks a logical progression of facts. Applying the IBC (Introduction, Body, Conclusion) format clarifies the request.

> (introduction) We can bring in the _____ project on time, save money, and be ready to market it by this fall if we combine resources with _____ Company, which is working to develop the same project.
>
> (body) We can continue to develop it separately; however, only one of us is going to win. Even the winner is going to find itself in a difficult financial position because of the high cost of this particular unit. Although the market is promising, if we continue on our own, develop the unit, and even hit the industry prior to _____ Company, we will still have to sell _____ units to break even. With current industry consumption, it will take us more than six years to recoup costs and show a profit. If we combine with _____ Company, we may be looking at a unit

that can be marketed within the next 12 months, and can show a profit by the time it has been out two years.

(conclusion) Although not all the figures are in, I believe it would be to our benefit to form a joint research, development, and marketing team with _____ Company, and we should do it as soon as possible.

The AIDA (Attention, Interest, Desire, Action) format could also be used to improve the organization of the letter.

(attention) We have the opportunity to produce and market the project, and return a profit to the company within two years, if we combine resources with _____ Company.

(interest) _____ Company has been working on the project almost as long as we have, and from our information they have even developed some parts of the equipment with more state-of-the-art improvements than our unit. Their unit is reportedly running 10% less in cost, too. Our project is running behind and our costs are running almost 15% higher than anticipated. This means our finished product, when ready, will be the most expensive in the industry.

(desire) We have also heard that the _____ Company is having financial difficulties. The project is expensive and they may be looking for another company to share the burden with them. We would benefit from their engineering advancements, and they would benefit from our marketing expertise.

(action) I would like to suggest we contact _____ Company, and suggest a meeting. We can then discuss interests and perhaps come to an agreement that would benefit both of us.

8. GENERALITIES

One of the faults some letter writers suffer from is generalities; the presentation of broad statements instead of specific facts. Today's sophisticated, knowledgeable businessperson will not accept generalizations. Letters and memos must concentrate on specifics.

When purchasing a home, a buyer would ask the realtor questions like "How many bedrooms does it have?" "How many baths does it have?" "What is the electrical bill like?" "How much are the taxes?" "Where does the school district rank?" All specific questions requiring specific answers. The realtor may begin by saying, "This is a great house" (a very general statement) but ultimately, to sell the property, the agent is going to have to answer specific queries from the buyer. Letters need to be specific as well. Note the following two examples.

(general) It is usually conceded that the company that has the best research and development department will usually win when it comes to producing prototypes. Although there are exceptions, it is difficult to replace proven expertise, and the facility with the best R&D will usually come up with the solution.

(specific) Our R&D department has been involved in nearly 100 projects, and of those it has developed the selected product more than 90% of the time.

Specific letters cover facts and figures that are quantitative and measurable.

9. BREVITY

In the past, the length of a letter did not matter, as long as it was well put together and maintained the reader's interest. Today's reader has less time to devote to correspondence. Everyone wants to know the bottom line—now. Despite the length of the following letter, it holds the reader's attention and effectively states its purpose.

A person in your income bracket may have more complex financial needs than you recognize. Perhaps your current financial advisor or money manager has not pointed out some of the additional services and advisory programs you could benefit from. Perhaps he hasn't suggested tax-saving and investment strategies that others in your income or professional group are currently following. I am always disappointed when professionals only react and do not take the time to care about my needs ahead of time. Right now, we are looking at the most volatile financial climate in the history of our company. Preserving wealth and planning are difficult.

Come tax time, all the recommendations in the world will not help. The time to develop your investment strategy is now.

If you would like, I would be willing to spend an hour or two with you without any compensation or fee. I would propose we examine your financial situation, review your last year's taxes, and look at your goals. I would ask you a number of questions, and even recommend strategies. I'll do it as a service to you. I would be delighted if you wanted to retain me after our meeting, but don't feel obligated.

I've helped many people in situations similar to yours, and I believe I could help you. Perhaps my advice would be an eye opener; perhaps not. I have found that many people, who believe they have their tax and investment matters in hand, suddenly begin to wonder about their situation, when I pose certain questions.

If I can help you, it could represent a savings of thousands or even tens of thousands of dollars that you could put in the bank. It would be money you could save, invest, and enjoy. It could change your entire thinking about taxes and investments.

I have some innovative (but legal!) investment ideas that are much more dynamic and unusual than many planners. My practice has grown because of those ideas and the results I have obtained for my clients.

If you are wondering just how much I can do for someone in your situation, call or send in the enclosed card. I will get back to you. Or, drop by at your convenience. However, because of my schedule, I would suggest you arrange for an appointment first.

What can you lose? Better yet, think of how much you can win, and there is no obligation.

This letter keeps the reader's attention for a couple of reasons—it addresses needs (making and saving money) and offers benefits (investment growth and tax savings). The letter can be divided easily into either an AIDA or an IBC format.

The rule: say what you have to say as quickly and as pointedly as possible. Although the example letter is long, it is not redundant. The writer does not keep making the same promises. He carefully takes the reader through the offer and sells him at the same time.

10. ASSUMPTIONS

You can lose your readers by assuming they know all of the facts or figures. Whenever putting correspondence together, it never hurts to repeat something that was stated in a previous letter or conversation. Restating pertinent facts eliminates misunderstandings or doubts.

11. TONE, DIRECTION, AND STRATEGY

A letter should be no different than a conversation with a business associate. Conversations usually begin with small talk about a nonbusiness subject, and then proceed to business. The nonbusiness portion of the conversation helps develop rapport and understanding. Letters require the same handling. A friendly opening gives the recipient a sense of familiarity with the writer, and the feeling that what follows is more than just words on paper. The feeling conveyed by the letter is the tone.

Writers should be aware that anything on paper projects a tone and an attitude. Words have their own meaning, but the tone in which they are presented creates their impact. The following letter was sent from an engineer to a prospect. Although the content is business, the engineer manages to use words that convey a sense of humor and friendliness. The letter, which is brief, light, and amusing followed a meeting between the engineer and the prospect, in which the engineer presented a proposal.

> I enjoyed the opportunity of meeting with you and partaking in some lively and exciting conversation on the art of information technology.
>
> I scoured my vault and found a copy of the book we discussed, and I am sure you will find Dr. Einstein's comments quite amusing in the light of where we have gone in the past half-century.
>
> My regards to your assistant, and my thanks to both of you for an enjoyable evening.

The engineer makes the most out of language by using some not-so-common terms such as "partaking" and "scoured my vault." The letter showed the client that the engineer was approachable.

OTHER PITFALLS

The common mistakes discussed in this chapter are not the only reasons requests and proposals fail. In today's competitive business environment, politics, personality, and psychology impact the effectiveness of correspondence.

Letter writing is not what it once was. Corporate downsizing has created a more competitive attitude. The motivations and intentions of the letter writer are not always apparent. A suggestion letter to peers within a marketing department, sent by the advertising director, might appear to be an innocent act designed to help others. But if the letter writer secretly sends a copy of the letter to the senior vice president in charge of marketing, it becomes a correspondence designed to showcase the advertising director's capabilities in running other areas. The actual motive of the letter is never evident to the marketing department peers.

Employees can be driven to make political moves by ambition, position justification, job protection, or dozens of other reasons.

No one in business is immune to the political game. Thus, when memos and letters are sent, political ramifications should be considered. Taking the time to think about the possible results is a good reason to hold letters and memos for a day before sending them. Do you want political reverberations or is there another way to get the message across without rocking the high rise?

An engineer at a software company was given the responsibility of developing a product that the distributors would embrace. The engineer was under enormous pressure to move fast. However, he did his research before he went to the design stage. The engineer talked to numerous distributors, gathered input and comments, and asked them what they thought their customers would buy and what they thought would sell.

The engineer also talked to the marketing department within his company. He did not, of course, *have* to go to his own marketing department. But the engineer knew that having the marketing staff behind him would give his product a greater chance of success.

Politically, the engineer made the correct move. When it comes time to obtain support for a new product, service, or procedure, people within a company are not enamored with change. Getting them to accept the idea before they are introduced to the process increases the chances for success.

Politics is not new within companies. More than 30 years ago, a producer in England was trying to get his product introduced into the United States via an American subsidiary. He talked constantly to his counterparts at the U.S. company, told them how successful the product was in Europe, and suggested the U.S. company could also do well if it introduced the product.

The U.S. company was resistant to change, and the English producer tried unsuccessfully for nearly two years to get his counterparts to accede to his request. Finally, he went to his boss, presented his case, discussed the marketing possibilities, the increased sales the company would get by utilizing the U.S. market, and the additional profits. His boss took the suggestion up the corporate ladder and, within weeks, the American counterparts were told to release the product and market it.

As a result, the Beatles—one of the most successful recording acts in the history of the music industry—were introduced to America. The company (EMI) made millions, and the producer's American counterparts were eventually asked to leave because management, both in the United States and England, had lost confidence in their ability.

OTHER POINTS TO REMEMBER

Another corporate element of letter writing is personality. Everyone is different, and the astute letter writer keeps the recipient in mind when composing correspondence. Put yourself in the recipient's position, and get people the recipient respects to endorse your suggestion.

Respected opinions can do a great deal to soften personalities and make them more pliable to ideas. Here is one way someone else's name can help. An aggressive job applicant investigates a company and finds that there are no openings. The applicant does some research and comes up with an idea that could benefit the company. The applicant puts the idea in writing and sends it to the chief executive officer of the company.

The CEO reads the suggestion, but has no idea if it is viable. The CEO sends the suggestion letter, along with a note, to the head of the department that the idea would impact. The department head would probably have thrown the idea away if it had not come with a note from the CEO. Instead, the department head calls the applicant in for an interview.

The applicant has cleverly worked around the department head's personality with an "endorsement" from the company's top official, the CEO. Working the personality from a different angle resulted in an interview.

Benjamin Disraeli, the 19th-century British Prime Minister, once said, "My idea of an agreeable person is a person who agrees with me." Many executives have the same opinion. In order to create a successful letter or memo suggesting change, keep in mind that people have a natural resistance to change. In addition to respected opinions, you may need to use psychology.

Nearly every letter and memo has a psychological impact. Thank-you notes stir feelings of gratitude, and letters of criticism can create feelings of resentment.

There are ways to produce the psychological impact you desire while reducing animosity and resentment. Remember, letters that dwell on the negative are going to be resented. If you are in a position where something must be criticized, incorporate some good elements.

The following letter was written by an ambitious engineer who wanted to move from engineering to marketing. The engineer had done a good analysis of the sales failure of one of the company's airplanes, and had stated it well. Despite the accuracy of the analysis, the engineer was never given an interview, nor invited to talk to the marketing director, because the entire letter was negative. The letter was an indictment of the marketing and design departments. The points might have been correct, but no one appreciates being torn down.

> In analyzing our _____ product, it was obvious to me that one of the problems is the design, and the second is the price and sales approach. If you examine our competition, their model is more aerodynamic and the price is 8% below ours.
>
> Since design takes at least five years to modify in our industry and with our equipment, I recommend we concentrate on the possibilities of reducing the price. Later, we can turn our attention to the design.
>
> My first step would be to . . . .

The letter was sent to the CEO, the vice president in charge of design, marketing executives, and accounting. The design vice president was not pleased. The engineer makes some bold statements without citing any proof.

To avoid offending the recipient of a critical letter, it is necessary to blend the good with the bad. Toastmasters, an organization that specializes in helping executives and others improve their speaking skills, does an excellent job at blending. When a member gives a talk, there is always an evaluator. The evaluator's job is to critique the speaker; however, the person offering the criticism follows these guidelines: "There are good things in every talk . . . point them out . . . offer suggestions . . . do not condemn."

Even if someone gives a disastrous speech, the evaluator will find something good to say. The negative is introduced along with the positive comments. The same technique can be utilized to make letters and memos more effective. Criticism is easy; making critical comments in a positive way is where the difficulty comes in. The more critical the correspondence, the greater the resistance and the less chance you have of getting your message across. The next chapter examines the memo, another written document that concerns many executives.

Chapter 4

The Seventeen Most Common Memo Mistakes—and Additional Advice

There is but one art—to Omit.

Robert Louis Stevenson

Writers who practice brevity, conciseness, and organization compose the best memos. Good memos are planned and outlined. The key to an effective memo is getting the reader's attention—immediately.

Although the AIDA (Attention, Interest, Desire, Action) and IBC (Introduction, Body, Conclusion) approaches enable the author of a memo to garner the reader's attention, the formulas do not guarantee that the memo will be brief. Many of the mistakes that can destroy a memo are similar to the errors that ruin letters, but some are primarily mistakes made by memo writers.

1. THE "INSIDE" TRAP

Even though a memo is going to stay within the company, the writer cannot assume that all of the readers will know what the acronyms or jargon mean. The fastest way to lose readers is to confuse them. The following memo could lose nontechnical readers because of the acronyms and jargon.

Training for the DCX course is going to be limited to attendees from the Weidner Facility, unless the person desiring registration has gone through ACA and ACB pretechnology briefings. Those in other facilities may have gone through Tri-X briefings as well.

Everyone reading the memo may know these terms, but the writer can't be sure. Each term should be explained, as in this revised memo.

> Training for the DCX (PC technology) course is going to be limited to only those from the Weidner Facility, unless those outside Weidner who want to attend have gone through ACA and ACB pretechnology briefings. ACA, which is known as basic PC reprogramming, troubleshooting, and problem solving, and ACB, which is advanced PC problem solving, are sometimes called Tri-X training. DCX is advanced PC training, and anyone wanting to enroll should have gone through one of the other courses first. If you need additional clarification or information, contact HR.

The revised memo clears up doubts and is a good example of basic letter writing for the lowest common denominator; writing so the person with the least understanding of the subject will comprehend what is being said.

The following memo is clear to the readers only if they happen to know the acronyms and the definitions of the technical terms. Two-thirds of the audience for this memo were nontechnical and did not know what BP or Visual Matrix meant.

> The implementation of REA-Net provides us with many benefits such as improved storage, maintenance, and communication of information. With the advent of BP, Visual Matrix, and Executive Information System, much of our critical business information is now stored in electronic formats.

2. CONCISENESS

Do not take two pages to say what can be said in one. Go back through your memo to see whether it can be cut. A shorter memo has a much better chance of being read. The following memo contains excessive wording.

> Management has gone to a great deal of trouble to ensure that all our information is adequately protected, especially the data that is on our electronic systems. This data in many cases is confidential and should not be shared with everyone. The purpose of your password is to keep confidential information confidential. Do not share your password with others. Employees who do share their password are violating their contract with the company. Any

employee who does not obey these rules will be subject to disciplinary measures.

The revised memo gets the message across in a clear and concise manner.

> Passwords are not to be shared among staff members, copied, or left in a conspicuous place. Passwords should be changed occasionally to reduce the risk of unauthorized use. Employees who violate these rules are subject to disciplinary procedures.

Short memos are generally the best choice, but sometimes a long, well-written memo is necessary. The following memo excerpt was from an information technology professional to senior management. The memo represented a report; however, the technology professional who put it together did some excellent outline work. There are five summaries plus closing comments, which make the document easy to read. The writer also varied type styles, another technique that eases the reader through a lengthy document.

> <u>(summary)</u> The _____ focus group team completed four weeks of travel to four different affiliate locations. This document summarizes the meetings and various comments regarding the _____ program heard during the focus group meetings, and during our stay with the affiliates. Because this document will be distributed to various _____ staff, I have provided both summary and detail information. I trust this will serve to provide the sales team with valuable information and ideas about the _____ initiative to use when talking to prospective affiliates. The support team will get a better idea of the potential impact of _____ for both large and small companies, and the frank feedback to _____ from the attendees of our sessions.
>
> The information I have included in this document is confidential: several suggestions and comments pertaining to version 2.0, as well as the status of plans for several affiliates, are summarized. Please do not provide copies of this document to anyone but _____ staff, and be selective and careful about your communication of this information.

The initial executive summary tells management what information the memo contains. The reader has the option of preceding or dropping the memo, but the writer has done a good job of keeping management interested. The confidentiality statement is another element that, while emphasizing the sensitivity of the material, will draw most people through the document. In the complete memo, the writer lists results from one group meeting. The results, which go on for several pages are introduced with a summary.

> The four-day session was attended by 14 people each day. A single office attended all four days and provided the information that went into the focus group report. The purpose of the focus group was to ascertain the reaction of users to the cost of the _____ software and hardware. This company is regarded as typical of many of our mid-size affiliates, and if they deemed the program (and the hardware) too expensive, we would have to re-think our plan. Based on information gathered during the four days, and the cost model that was presented to the group, they unanimously decided that the software and the hardware cost were within reason.

3. DOUBLE-SPACING

Single-spaced memos are difficult to read. A full page of single-spaced material is discouraging to readers. The more difficult the material is to read, the less likely it is that the recipient will absorb the information. With time always being a concern, a memo that appears dense is likely to be put aside for another time. Double-spacing is a better way to get your readers' attention.

4. PARAGRAPH LENGTH

Memo writers have a tendency to put together extremely long sentences that flow into longer paragraphs. If a memo is longer than a half-page when double-spaced, it would probably benefit from breaking it up into shorter paragraphs. Several short paragraphs appear less difficult to read than one long paragraph. One way to break up a memo is to include headlines or subheads.

> *MEETING NOTES* [a large subhead or headline]
>
> A critical issue at _____ is to decide whether to use the software system remotely via phone dial-up, or by downloading data to a portable computer.
>
> I. Downloading [a second-rank headline]
>   (1) A current project of the _____ will provide a new tool to associates to download listing information.

Using capital letters, boldface, and underlining aids the reader. Do not use too many capital letters in a row [A SUMMARY OF IN-FORMATION FOR SENIOR MANAGEMENT] because it is difficult to read. Use all capital letters only when you are highlighting two or three words.

5. NEEDS ASSESSMENT

When writing, keep in mind the people who will receive the memo. What do they want to know? What matters to them? Make the memo pertinent to the readers. If you are proposing a reorganization of your area, explain how it will impact the readers' area. People are concerned with how something is going to affect their lives. Even though you may have to give background information and explain why the changes are coming, you still have to address the recipients' needs. If the proposal is for a new technology initiative, explain what impact the initiative will have on the recipients, what their involvement will be, and so on. The following memo explains what is going to happen and how it will affect those receiving the memo.

> Our decision to revise the software in the home office PCs was made in order to increase efficiency. Those at the home office with the _____ software can expect downtime of between three to five hours this Friday afternoon, starting at 3 P.M. We chose Friday because of the alternate work schedule that many employees are on, and at that time of the day (and day of the week), it would cause a minimum of inconvenience.

6. BENEFITS

When proposing a change, the purchase of equipment, or the addition of staff, remember to clearly explain the benefits to your area, your department, your company, and the customers. The benefits should overshadow any dollar figures.

> The change in software, although inconvenient, will enable every department to obtain information up to 15% sooner than they get it presently.

7. MONEY REQUESTS

Requesting funds is always delicate. When making the request, explain why the money is needed, how much money is needed, and how the money will be spent. Describe the benefits of what your requesting before you state the price. The person reading the correspondence is going to have some reaction to the price. You do not want that reaction to cloud his or her thinking before you can point out the reasons for the expenditure.

Conversely, if the memo is discussing a cost savings, put the amount saved at the beginning.

> We are presently spending more than $2,500 a month for vendors who park in front of the building and obtain a validation from us. We can save that money and, at the same time, provide parking for vendors and other visitors by following the simple procedure of having all visitors park in the rear structure, where our rates are greatly reduced.

8. EMOTIONS

Emotion may help sell in person, but it does little good on the written page. Stick to the facts and the benefits to educate, convince, and sell the recipient. The memo does not have to be flat and colorless, but use adjectives sparingly.

9. OPINION-MAKERS

Before writing a memo requesting change, get the thoughts of the leading opinion-makers in your department or company. Opinion-makers are those individuals who have a great deal of influence over others. Bounce your idea off opinion-makers who can offer valuable input and give you a new perspective on the proposal. If they like the proposal, they could turn out to be champions of your idea.

10. THE BASICS

Incorrect spelling and punctuation may not destroy your memo but they could cause the recipient to think that the idea the memo is relaying is not important. The basics have impact on memos. Incorrect spelling might suggest you don't care much about the thoughts contained in the memo.

11. PREACHING

Let people reach their own conclusions. In a memo, stay away from statements such as "Any reasonable person can see . . . " or "It is obvious that the only way we can do this . . . " Statements that take decision-making away from the recipient say, "If you do not agree with me, there must be something wrong with you." People want to make their own decisions. If the memo writer lays out the ground-work, provides the data, and states the case objectively, the recipient will probably agree. Using didactic wording in an attempt to sway the reader seldom works.

12. TOPIC DRIFTING

Memos require having a clear, planned direction and a discussion of only one subject. The following memo drifts from subject to subject.

> During our Network Support meeting, several items were brought up that need clarification. Involving the advertising department was the subject of co-op funds. The technology area had the dilemma of addressing a multitude of systems that had to be put to-gether in order for our Affiliates to communicate with us, and the marketing area had posed numerous questions about the approach we were taking with brochures. Additionally, the meeting and plan-ning area had to design a program for the international convention planned for next March.
>
> My initial thoughts on these subjects were for the meeting and planning area to sit with the marketing department in order to de-sign the proper brochures . . . .

This executive would have been better off addressing the issues in separate memos. Combining several topics leads to confusion.

13. FORMAL LANGUAGE

Engineers and scientists have the ability to talk in plain, easy-to-understand English. However, when writing memos, many profes-sionals have a tendency to use five-syllable words and formal language that sounds alien.

14. BREVITY

Making paragraphs too long, and sentences too complex, reduces the chances that your memo will be read and understood. Strive for brief sentences and short paragraphs. Long, involved paragraphs can read like passages from a Faulkner novel. Remember, we live in a sound bite society.

15. WORD PROCESSORS

Thanks to computers and word processing programs, a page of solid type can be broken up, points can be bulleted, titles can be set in all capital letters, text can be underlined or boldfaced, and a variety of type faces can be used. Well-written memos have copy that almost jumps off the page because the writer has taken the time to bullet and highlight key points.

16. INDIVIDUALITY

Even if a memo is being sent to many different people, the key to writing good correspondence is writing as if it were going to just one person. Writing to the individual forces you to make the memo more personal. Memos become impersonal when the material is written for a group rather than an individual.

17. CONCLUSIONS

Let the reader know what you want. The recipient should know that you want an action taken, or you want a budget to be approved, or you want a process to be discarded, or you want your department to be given additional funds. Whatever the purpose, make sure there is no doubt about what the memo is requesting.

MEMO CATEGORIES

Most memos fall into one of the following categories.

Thanks

Reminders and requests

Business recaps

Congratulations

Proposals

Reports

Memos in any category can be either formal or informal. Informal correspondence is characterized by contractions and by adjectives that convey a sense of familiarity. Words such as "delightful" and "heartfelt" make a memo familiar and friendly. Pronouns can make correspondence more informal, too. The following memo could be classified as formal.

To accomplish our objectives, we have realigned several of the departments while focusing and broadening responsibility levels to get the job done. This new architecture should be of significant benefit in helping all departments. The first step in focusing a team of people in a uniform direction is the establishment of a single goal. We developed a mission statement for the team:

The _____ team commits to providing consistently excellent technology, training, research products, programs, and services that will result in our being a valuable addition to the corporate structure.

The following is an informal memo:

We're on the cutting edge—again! The technical services group is in the process of upgrading all computers that will be used to access the 1996 budget model. We'll be installing the latest version of Excel 5.0. If a technical services representative has not contacted you, one will shortly. The rep will schedule a convenient time for the upgrade of your machine. Now, how's this for a service promise: it will not take longer than one hour for the upgrade. If it does, we will buy you a burger at McDonald's!

Deciding which style of memo is appropriate depends on the occasion, the familiarity of the writer with the audience, and the memo's message. The formal memo example, which was setting a direction for an entire department, required a more serious tone. The informal memo example was taking a serious subject—downtime on the computer—and making it lighter.

The following memos abide by the rules given in this chapter. They have been selected for their diverse approaches.

To:
From:
Date:
Subject: Confidentiality of Information

Information Technology is continuing to review our internal workstation and network security to ensure that proper controls and procedures are in place to protect critical business information. It is equally important for each of you to ensure that proper security measures are being followed by each member of your staff or department, and that they all know the importance of passwords and the need to protect. The following guidelines will assist in this goal:

1. When accessing sensitive information, employees must not leave documents or spreadsheets "open" while workstations are unattended. Similarly, workstations logged into a corporate information system must not be left unattended. When leaving an office or workplace, close all documents and log off all active applications.
2. Information that is confidential or sensitive should not be sent via E-mail unless it is sent as an attached document or spreadsheet that is password-protected.
3. All budgetary, salary, and other confidential information should be protected by adding a password when created or saved.
4. Passwords are not to be shared among staff members. Passwords should be changed on an occasional basis to reduce the risk of unauthorized access.

Please make sure that all staff is familiar with these guidelines. To aid in the protection of sensitive and confidential information, I have attached procedures for assigning passwords to documents and files. I have also attached a list of passwords that should be avoided, because they are too familiar to most in our industry. Should you or your staff need help with the use of these procedures, please contact Information Technology.

Confidentiality memo.

Note: This memo uses the IBC format. The last paragraph is the conclusion, with the middle part building toward it, and the opening is a paraphrase of the conclusion. This update from the information technology department to employees, explains the importance of confidentiality in the aerospace and other defense-oriented industries. Information in the nondefense sector can be equally as sensitive.

To:
From:
Date:
Subject: Congratulations are in order!

Congratulations to Sylvester _____ , who is the proud recipient of a $50 gift certificate to the Great Mall Center. Sylvester was awarded this certificate for submitting a suggestion for our Rideshare Program. Sylvester's idea was to incorporate the use of hang tags for our carpoolers.

We will implement this procedure starting next week. The following changes will be made in the event any employee who carpools to work wishes to take advantage of the reserved parking spaces for carpoolers.

1. All vehicles utilizing the carpooler reserved parking spaces must have a valid registered carpooler hang tag displayed on the rearview mirror or the dashboard.
2. Hang tags will be issued on a quarterly basis.
3. Hang tags can be obtained by completing the carpool registration form and submitting it to administrative services.
4. Carpool registration forms can be obtained from the receptionist or the hot files located in the commuter information centers on each floor.

We have had a problem with non _____ employees parking in the reserved spaces, and this new procedure will eliminate that problem. Please note that _____ Parking will be ticketing all cars parked in our reserved carpool spaces that do not have the hang tag displayed. If you are a carpooler, please be sure and obtain your tag. We will not start ticketing, however, until the week of July 10.

A congratulatory memo properly structured.

To:
From:
Date:
Subject: Business Disaster Recovery Plan

I am in the process of creating and implementing a Business Disaster Recovery Plan (BDRP) for the _____ office. Since we want to ensure that all facets of business recovery will be addressed in this Plan, it is important that I receive feedback and information from each of you.

In the event the office becomes unusable due to fire or some other disaster, the BDRP will specifically identify the action to be taken to resume business in a contingency mode until (1) our current office space is restored to usable condition or (2) an alternate site is identified and prepared as new offices.

Assumptions:

1. The _____ Center building is a total loss, either temporarily or permanently.
2. Critical business will be conducted in contingency mode at a temporary site for up to 60 days.
3. Critical business is defined as any function necessary for the continuation of business while operating in contingency mode.
4. Primary or alternate vendors will be available to assist in the recovery process.
5. All vital records are stored in secure, off-site locations and are accessible immediately following the disaster.
6. Restoration and recovery of the computer system is addressed in a different document.

Based on these assumptions, please address the following:

1. Identify critical business functions in your department.
2. Identify the number of staff, along with general responsibilities, necessary to perform these critical business functions.
3. Identify critical forms/documentation.
4. Identify critical equipment and supplies.
5. In addition, identify any classified bio-tech products under test.

Please provide this information by Wednesday, November 14.

Business disaster recovery plan memo.

Note: In view of natural disasters, many companies are preparing "business disaster recovery plans." These plans are useful in firms where stored information is vital to the functioning of the company.

To:
From:
Date:
Subject: Signature Responsibilities and Contract Authorization

A critical element of any company control structure is the delegation of signing authority—that is, those who have the assigned responsibility to commit the company legally. We wanted to take an opportunity to stress _____ position with regard to the importance of proper signatory requirements.

At the very fiber of _____ policies exists the Delegation of Authority Guidelines (DAG). This is the foundation on which the Board of Directors has empowered our President to delegate various levels of authority throughout the company. All expenses and contracts must be properly authorized as delineated in the DAG. Only actual signatures are acceptable, and it is against company policy for someone to sign another individual's name for authorization purposes. Documents requiring authorizations that do not have the proper signatures will not be processed.

Due to heavy travel assignments or other conflicts, we recognize that there may be occasions when obtaining an actual signature is not practical, given certain time constraints. Following are general guidelines to follow under the circumstances described.

Expenses

1. Airline tickets will not be issued unless properly authorized. For rush trips, the authorization authority is expanded as follows:
   a. For travel requests only, both _____ and _____ have been delegated authority.
   b. If necessary, _____ can approve the issuance of an urgent ticket.
2. For general expenses, if the proper signatory individual is not available and something has to be done, it is allowable to get

Signature responsibilities and contract authorization memo.

Note: One of the most sensitive areas for any company is the responsibility of signing for goods and services. The following memo covers this problem.

the signature of another employee who has the proper level of signing authority.

3. For travel expenses, _____ policy requires that reimbursement to employees must be authorized by a superior in the employee's reporting hierarchy.

Contracts

All contracts must be signed by an officer of the company, because a corporation can only be bound to a contract by an officer. If _____ does not have an officer executing a contract, we may have difficulty enforcing the contract. In addition, all contracts must be reviewed by Legal prior to signing. The Legal review is to ensure that the language is appropriate and consistent with our policies.

Letters

If the signature is for general or routine correspondence, it is allowable to have the secretary/administrative assistant sign for the principal, based on verbal approval, but there should be clear identification, by initials, who actually signed the correspondence.

To:
From:
Date:
Subject: FAX BROADCAST ANALYSIS

One of the invoices I continue to reconcile and approve for payment each month is the MCI Fax broadcast. This is the service we have used for several years to send out fax broadcasts to the various distribution groups. I have noticed that the usage, and consequently the cost, for this service has increased lately. The attached nine-month analysis of MCI Fax broadcast usage was prepared to determine whether we have any opportunities for reducing these costs.

The first sheet attached is a breakdown by department; the second sheet reflects the amount of peak and nonpeak usage. Following are a few comments generated by the attached analysis.

1. The difference between the usage between _____ and _____ is significant. These two divisions may want to compare notes to see whether any cost savings can be generated.
2. _____ is a high user. Is there a more cost-effective way to disseminate _____ information and is the high volume of usage needed?
3. The cost of peak versus nonpeak usage. Currently, 44% of our transmissions are being sent at peak times. This results in a cost that is 43% higher than if those same transmissions had not been sent at a peak hour. It would be highly beneficial if each area would evaluate the possibility of reducing the number of messages sent during peak time. If anyone in your area needs assistance on the procedure for sending messages to be transmitted at nonpeak times, please contact _____ or _____ .
4. The volume of transmissions. Is the high volume of transmissions, and the frequency with which they are being sent, necessary and productive?

If you have any questions, or would like additional information, please do not hesitate to contact me.

Memo addressing expense increases.

Note: Some companies run into cost areas that suddenly begin to escalate. The following memo is an attempt by management to control escalating expenses. The memo makes employees aware of the problem, and provides a sheet reflecting each department's usage and expenditure.

Date:
To:
From:
Subject: Ethics Questionnaire

Attached is a copy of the company's ethics questionnaire. We conduct the survey each year to ensure that the guidelines outlined in the company's ethics statement are being followed. You have been selected because of your job level or because your job responsibilities expose you to confidential information about our company or customers.

When completing the questionnaire, please use the following to assist you in determining whether an issue is or appears to be in violation of the company's ethics statement:

1. Serving on the Board of a nonprofit organization does not need to be included in response to question number 1.
2. If you have previously submitted a potential conflict situation, including service on a Board at _____ request, and there was an appropriate approval, please note the date of prior approval and the name of the person approving the situation.

In addition to the two items listed above, you should read the footnotes in bold print that appear below several of the questions. They will further guide you in responding properly.

Finally, before signing the completed questionnaire, you should review the company's ethics statement entitled "_____ : Making the Right Choice." A typewritten copy of the ethics statement is attached in the event you have misplaced your original booklet. New booklets are being sent for distribution and will be given to each associate upon delivery to us.

Questionnaires must be completed as soon as possible, and returned no later than Monday, March 27.

Ethics questionnaire memo.

Note: Every company has ethical guidelines, and surveying employees on a yearly basis to ensure that proper ethics are in place is common practice. The following memo is the introduction to an ethics questionnaire.

The questions:

1. Were you, during the past year, while employed with
   _____ , a director, officer, employee, partner, or trustee
   of, or did you hold any other position with, any business enterprise (other than family business not doing business with the
   _____)?
2. Have you acted on behalf of the company or any of its sub-
   sidiaries during the past year in connection with any transaction in which you had a personal interest?
3. Did you or any family member living in your household have
   any investment involving an amount greater than 10% of your
   gross assets, or $10,000 if that amount is larger, or involving an
   ownership interest greater than 2% of the outstanding equity
   interest, in any business enterprise, that engaged in any business transaction with the company?
4. Did you or any family member living in your household borrow
   during the past year an amount greater than 10% of your gross
   assets, or $10,000 if that amount is larger, on an unsecured
   basis from any bank, financial institution, or other business
   that engaged in business transaction with the company?
5. Did you or any family member living in your household receive
   during the past year, directly or indirectly, a gift of more than
   insubstantial value in connection with any business involve-
   ments or transactions the company may have had?
6. Have you been involved in or are you aware of any situation
   where money, property, or services of the company were contributed or otherwise made available during the past year to
   political parties or candidates, or used to reimburse individuals for contributions they might have made?
7. Are you aware of any unlawful or improper conduct by others
   where funds or services, business gifts, gratuities, favors,
   bribes, or kickbacks were given or received by an employee of
   the company?
8. Were you involved in any other conflict-of-interest situation or
   are you aware of any such situation on the part of any
   employee?

To:

Date:

Subject: Purchase by _____ of _____

The news of _____ purchase of _____ surprised us this morning. The attached articles from the *New York Times* and *Wall Street Journal* give the sketchy details. Now, what is the potential impact of the transaction? Our perspective:

1. The two are a good match. Both are strong with the same audience and use the same demographic profile in their marketing efforts.
2. This is the third time the _____ has been sold in 20 years. This makes for a great deal of upheaval internally.
3. Is this the beginning of a trend? Will other companies from this industry enter our field and purchase companies? If so, what companies are the logical targets?
4. These two companies tied together could do a great deal of cross-selling.
5. Both companies are in diverse industries, but their customer base is similar. This is the key advantage.
6. Although the purchase may not be any immediate threat to our company, the mere fact companies are being bought and sold (and folded) in our industry is making employees nervous. We believe management should address this issue and talk to employees soon.

Memo requesting information on industry mergers.

Note: Every industry has consolidation, and sometimes those mergers send reverberations through an entire industry as well as the individual companies concerned. The following memo was issued shortly after a purchase, in which one of the largest companies in the industry was unexpectedly sold. An analysis was provided to senior management for evaluation.

Date:
To:
Subject: Vacation Time

Presently, vacations must be taken between (month) and (month). In the past, we have given all new employees a week's vacation during their first year even if they have not earned it by being here a year. Someone who left before completing the first year was charged back for the unearned vacation time.

There has been enormous confusion surrounding this policy, so we are changing it to a "vacation earned" policy. If you started in March, for instance, and want to take your vacation in June, you have earned three months toward your vacation. We would pay you for ¼ of one week's pay as vacation. If you started in November and want a vacation in August, you would have earned 10 months toward a week's vacation and will be paid for ⅚ of a week's pay, or 83%.

You must take your vacation within the year. You cannot accrue it. If you do not wish to take vacation, you will be paid for the days earned, if approved by management. Employees on the job for more than a year will not be impacted by this change.

Vacation policy memo.

Note: All employees are concerned with vacation. The following memo addresses a vacation policy.

Date:
To:
From:
Subject: Audit

Auditors from the accounting firm of (name) will be here (date, time) to inspect our inventory. In preparation, please be prepared to show the auditors all physical inventory. They will want to inspect and count all items, and you may also have to document the original purchase price.

    This is a key part of our fiscal year closing, so be prepared to assist (name of firm) in any way the auditors feel is necessary. If you have a question, please see your departmental vice presidents.

Audit memo.

Note: Audits are unpleasant for most companies because of the time they take. Whether the department is engineering, manufacturing, or accounting, audits are time-consuming and cumbersome. The following memo was put out in an attempt to ease disruption and to speed the audit.

Date:
To:
From:
Subject: Production Meeting Summary

The pros and cons of introducing a new line of _____ in January 1996, instead of April 1996, were discussed. All agreed that it would be best to move the intro away from the beginning of the year and toward the spring, for a more favorable buyer attitude.

Other reasons for bringing the new technology into play in April were (1) this is the season when we have more downtime, and it would behoove us to use our plants to capacity at this point rather than waiting and paying overtime in order to produce the same goods; (2) we would beat the competition's new models, which are not slated, according to our intelligence, to hit the market until the summer.

It was agreed that Forrest _____ would be responsible for scheduling; Harry _____ for market research and obtaining buyer opinions; Jim _____ for arranging for raw materials; Gerald _____ to interface with R&D and engineering to ensure that the quality problems have been solved.

The committee agreed to meet in two weeks to discuss assignment results and to evaluate whether the April date was still a go.

Production meeting summary memo.

Note: Meetings are commonplace in most companies, and the gatherings that are most efficient are those in which there is a summary of what was discussed and who will be responsible.

Date:
To:
From:
Subject: Suggestion

Your idea that we create an incentive for customers to upgrade their
_____ systems has been taken under consideration. We have
decided to offer owners of the system a ($) rebate, when they trade
their current _____ for a _____ .
    Your idea was superb and in recognition of it you will find a
check for ($)_____ enclosed.

Suggestion award memo.

Note: Employees are a company's best source of ideas, and suggestion awards and memos are commonplace.

Date:
To:
From:
Subject: Suggestion

Your suggestion that we recycle the trims from our vinyl production
has been analyzed and it is an extremely viable idea.
    This process, which will be implemented in six to eight weeks,
will result in a direct savings to our firm. We commend you for your
inventiveness!
    Please accept my congratulations on the adoption of your idea,
and our thanks for your enthusiastic attitude.

Suggestion thank-you memo.

Chapter 5

Boilerplate for Successful Memos

There are hundreds of different kinds of memos that engineers, scientists, and technical professionals write to members of their department or to other departments throughout their companies.

The following memo categories represent the most popular. Although many of these memos are project- or product-specific, most can serve as a boilerplate for similar memos.

Nearly all of these memos are either in an AIDA or IBC format, with a clear introduction, body, and conclusion.

With these memos as a template, you will be able to construct a memo for virtually any purpose.

After studying our tri-fold technology line, it seems apparent that we could save time, improve productivity, and upgrade quality with a few simple changes. I have outlined the changes in the attached grid, which will allow you to see how the line can be changed.

I estimate that with the changes we can cut 5% from our production time and come out with a more reliable unit. Naturally, cutting production time will raise our productivity and profitability.

If the plan sounds feasible, I would be happy to explain it in greater depth after work or during your spare time. Please let me know how you would like to proceed.

Memo suggesting a change in production procedure.

Note: An engineer has come up with a new way of doing things. The cover memo tells the plan, and the material that follows details the process. Avoid showing all the financial and production changes in a cover memo. The cover memo should include only the pertinent items and describe overall what the change will mean.

For the past week, I have had members of my department observing the assembly line in an effort to determine why we have such a high instance of damaged casings. After carefully evaluating the different areas of the line, it became obvious that there is a bottleneck at the (where). Instead of making a smooth transition around the L, the casings get hung up because of the sharpness of the turn. When they stall on the line, they collide with each other, and the force is such that it causes damage to the casing's exterior.

Our recommendation is to either space the casings six inches farther apart by readjusting the line, or have maintenance straighten the L curve. Either one of these steps can save us several thousand dollars a month in damaged goods.

Memo to management regarding production problem.

Note: The problem is outlined and the solution is given.

To: _____   From: _____
Subject: _____   Date: _____

Attached is the plan summary of (name) Plan incorporating current reserves. I have also attached summary schedules for the (name) Pit and Section (number or name) projects that are not yet drilled or modeled sufficiently to move them into a proven reserve category.

Our 19____ production of 528,000 ounces is very optimistic and is still planned because of overriding corporate production goals. It is contingent on being able to gain accelerated leach ounce production and much higher mill throughput than we achieved in 19____ . Ongoing modeling in the Megapit is indicating sooner-than-expected redox boundaries in Cut (number), which may cause additional negative impacts. A much more realistic ounce attainment figure for the year of 19____ is 512,000.

Memo reporting plan and actual results.

Note: Projections will not be met, but the reasons are given.

Since we started on the thruster problem, we have discovered several additional problems with the system that will take more time for us to resolve. I know you are under pressure; however, in order to complete the job and ensure that we will not have any other difficulties, I would like to request an extension of two weeks beyond our originally agreed-on deadline.

We intend to use the added time to double-check the system and to conduct troubleshooting in other parts of the unit. In the long run, the extension will ultimately save us time and money.

Please let me know your thoughts as soon as possible, and notify me of any problems we have in obtaining the extension. I hope, of course, that our new target date of Sept. 15 will be acceptable.

Thank you for your time and understanding.

Memo requesting time extension.

Note: This memo requests a time extension. The rationale for the extension is given, and the new due date is spelled out. The writer did not ask for an extension without giving reasons. The memo was specific, which is an important feature of any memo.

One of our key clients, _____ Industries, has been complaining about the poor finish in our (name) cabinets. We have looked into the matter, and determined that the material we have been purchasing from (name) Corp. does not have the ingredients needed to maintain a long-lasting, high-quality finish.

To remedy this situation, as of this afternoon, we are switching suppliers for the finishing material in the (name) cabinets. (name), Inc. is our new source and they will be delivering a special "luster gloss" that will be standard on all our cabinets. If you have any questions, please discuss it with your shift engineer.

Memo regarding service complaint solution.

Note: The decision has been made and a new ingredient will be utilized to resolve problems.

Your suggestion that we revise the way we track our projects was well received by senior management and is being studied by our implementation team. The cost savings measures were especially attractive, and everyone on the team, as well as senior management, would like to thank you for the time you put into the suggestion, and the care with which you put together the procedural steps.

I am extremely grateful that we have professionals on staff who care so much for the company. Should the suggestion be adapted, there will, of course, be an incentive award; however, whether or not the tracking project becomes a reality, I wanted you to know how much I appreciate your time, interest, and efforts.

Suggestion acknowledgment memo.

Note: This memo is from a senior manager to an engineer within one of the departments. Management expresses concern and appreciation for the time and effort the employee put into the suggestion.

Your suggestion that we recycle the trims from our vinyl production has been analyzed and it is an extremely good idea. This recycling process, which will be implemented in six to eight weeks, will result in a direct savings to our firm, as well as a way to help preserve our environment.

My congratulations on this excellent idea and the adoption of your suggestion. Employees like you have helped make (name of company) the high-quality, caring, service-oriented company that it has become.

Suggestion thank-you memo.

Note: A good suggestion deserves a timely answer. Employees like to see whether—and when—their ideas are going to be implemented.

To: _____   From: _____

Subject: _____   Date: _____

We have conducted the following formal training since the merger:

1. *HITACHI HYDRAULIC SHOVEL OPERATION*
   Dates: October 26–30, 19____
   Hours of instruction: 6 hrs classroom, 44 hrs OJT
   Instructor: (name)
   Number of attendees: 26 had 1 hr of classroom
                            19 had 2–3 hours each of OJT

2. *BLASTING SEMINAR—2 SESSIONS*
   Dates: October 12–15 & October 18–21, 19____
   Hours of instruction: 24 hrs
   Instructor: (name)
   Number of attendees: 31

3. *NEVADA STATE BLASTING CERTIFICATION*
   Date: November 19, 19____
   Hours of instruction: 8 hrs
   Instructor: (name)

If there is any additional information you need, please let me know.

Training update memo.

Note: Straight-to-the-point memo about training.

For the past three months, I have been studying the manner in which we handle the tracking and progress of our new projects, and it occurred to me that we could save a great deal of time and be more accurate if we implemented a simple time management grid (draft enclosed).

Notice the grid has several key elements that our present system lacks. First, we are able to list and track every project on one central board. At a glance, we can determine the status of any one of them. Next, the system details major decision and cutoff dates. Occasionally, we are so busy that we miss cutoffs or decision periods. Once we do, we are obligated to go ahead or pay the vendor cancellation fees. This grid will enable us to save money and avoid many embarrassing issues.

I hope this idea meets with management's approval. I would be happy to answer any questions or to supply additional project grids to show how simply the system operates.

Idea memo from engineer to company.

Note: A time- and money-saving suggestion by an employee. This idea was adopted, and part of the reason for its acceptance was the simplicity in which it was explained. At times, engineering and/or technical areas of companies use complex jargon or language to explain things. This engineer kept the suggestion simple so that the human resources director could understand it.

It is with great pleasure that I learned today that the senior management committee has accepted your idea for the "time board," and will implement it companywide starting this Spring.

The creativity and thought you put into it were evident, and will prove to be of enormous benefit to the company. My sincere congratulations to you for this important new suggestion, and a special "extra thanks." It is one thing to see new suggestions originating from other departments; however, when the idea comes from my department, I am especially pleased and proud.

Enclosed you will find a check, which represents a small token of our company's appreciation for your efforts.

Suggestion appreciation memo.

Note: A memo congratulating an employee within the department for an award-winning suggestion.

Next Monday, we will hold our annual strategic planning departmental meeting, and the gathering gives us an excellent platform on which to change the way we are doing things, introduce new innovative techniques, and brainstorm together.

In today's tight, highly competitive environment, strategic planning is more than simply repeating and updating last year's plan. This year, I am asking each of you to bring your engineering "think caps" and ideas. This year, more than ever, I need your assistance in putting together a plan that will not only take us through next year, but one that will point the way for future years.

To start things off, we will have a creative session run by (name). You may remember (first name) from our convention, where he gave a highly enlightening speech on creativity. (First name) will be facilitating things throughout the day, and he has asked me to let all of you know that "anything goes." No ideas are too far out. You do not have to bring anything, except your creativity.

I look forward to seeing each of you at the Westin, and I am confident this year's planning and idea session will surpass anything we have ever done before.

Memo soliciting creative ideas from staff.

Note: The department head describes the planning process—and the openness—of a scheduled meeting. The memo is designed to stimulate the creative process in the group, and to get them to look at things differently.

Strategic planning is about to begin!

Before any of you groan, let me tell you how this year's session will differ from anything we have ever done.

Senior management has given us permission to examine our area, completely revamp it, and even throw away last year's plan. We are starting fresh, with new ideas.

To help with our new look, I am asking each of you to write a short memo and submit it to me by the end of next week (Oct. 28). In the memo, I would like you to list your thoughts on who our customers are and what products and services we can best devise to serve them.

Your memos will then become the basis for our planning meeting. If you believe that all our present products and services suffice, then say so. If you think we need revisions, write that down, too. This is a meeting where there will be no "wrong answers," only "right and good new ideas."

The all-day meeting, incidentally, will start with a continental breakfast at 8:00, and at 8:30 we will begin. I have enclosed an agenda, which will give you an idea of how different this year's meeting is going to be.

Once you examine the agenda, if you have any thoughts about changes or additions, please let me know. Remember, we want this to be the most open and creative meeting of the year, because it is the most important of the year.

Memo to staff regarding upcoming planning meeting.

Note: A department head stimulating staff for ideas.

Attached are the preliminary assignments for the (name) technical review. We will need to target completion of this document by early December, although we will have to prepare an intermediate presentation by mid-September for management and the policy committees. This is to determine whether (name) may continue to be capitalized.

We will review this, including more detailed timetables, at the August 14, 19____ , (name) development meeting in Albuquerque.

Based on positive feedback from the mines, I have arranged to have (name) conduct a one-day slope-stability seminar in (city) on August 11, 19____ . We had a similar session a few years back and found it beneficial not only for the mine planning and geology technical staff but also very informative for production supervisors, loader/shovel operator/trainers, and key members of the drill and blast crews. I have attached an outline of topics that will be covered.

I have reserved a meeting room in the West Hall of the (name) Convention Center starting at 7:30 A.M. with coffee and doughnuts. The seminar will run from 8:00 A.M. to 5:00 P.M., and an on-site lunch will be catered.

I have tentatively planned for 40 to attend, but that number is flexible. I do need a final count to give to the caterer by mid-July, so, by July 10th, please provide me with a final list of those planning to attend from your mine or project.

Memo regarding upcoming planning meeting.

Note: Dates are spelled out, as well as purpose.

Our long-awaited (name) planning meeting is almost here. On August 23–24, we will begin a two-day session designed to steer our department through 19____ . For the planning meeting, we will discuss all projects and services, set priorities, and determine (company name) prime goals for each division.

I expect numerous proposals to be made for changing our operation, and invite each of you to bring any ideas, regardless of how different, to this meeting.

Memo regarding upcoming planning meeting.

Note: Whether it describes a strategic planning meeting or something else, this memo is typical of those sent within a department to get employees thinking about an important planning event and what their role should be.

September 2, 19____
Page 1

Please find attached my thoughts to aid you in preparing a compilation prior to our next meeting. If you have any questions, feel free to call me at home in (where), where I will be from May 27 through June 4th. I would also appreciate it if you would call me after consolidating your input. I would like the opportunity to review those materials prior to the June 5th meeting. I have a FAX board in my home computer that can receive your input, but I would need to set it up just prior to your sending the FAX. My home phone number is _____ .

Checklist Items (may apply to all categories; level of detail differs)

1. *General.*
   General location—nearby mines/towns, climate?
   Access to property—road quality, distances?
   Infrastructure—nearby towns, utilities, transportation?
   Land ownership—mineral and surface rights, fractional
       ownership, government vs. private, royalties?
   Environmental constraints—endangered species in area,
       proximity to sensitive areas, regulatory requirements?
   Literature available—geologic reports, annual reports,
       permits, feasibility reports?

2. *Ore Reserve Data Base.*
   Geology—regional and local geology, alteration, oxidation,
       structural controls?
   Existing drillholes—number, type (RC, rotary, core, air), angle,
       depth, spacing, diameter, recovery, sample preparation
       procedures, assay procedures (AA, fire assay, check assays)?
   Effect of drilling on grade—differences between grades
       derived from different drilling techniques, sample
       contamination below the water table, systematic relation-
       ships between grade and recovery, factors used to reconcile
       grades obtained by different techniques?

Memo helping to set up agenda items for meeting.

Note: A thorough subject list for company that specializes in mining. The format has application for other planning meetings.

Density—methods used, number of determinations, variability?

Rock characteristics—hardness, grindability?

Moisture content—pump tests during drilling, lab measurements?

Metallurgical characteristics—refractory, mineralolology?

3. *Block Model Parameters.*

General description—baseline survey information, limits, orientation, block size (rationale for fixing dimensions)?

Input data—grade types/ranges of items needing to be tracked, accuracy required, data checking procedures?

Compositing criteria—minimum interval length, minimum number of samples required?

Geologic/mineralogic domains—how many, what is needed, level of detail required?

Density—wet or dry used, global or block-by-block attribute?

Process attributes—grinding index, recovery curves, clay content?

4. *Mining, Process, Equipment (current/prior operations).*

History—previous geology/mining operations?

Pit location and size?

Bench heights and optimizations?

Haul roads—widths/grades?

Mining rates?

Stripping, waste disposal, stockpiling?

Mine equipment fleet, age, condition?

Process description including tailings disposal?

Environmental controls, reclamation plans?

Manpower requirements?

September 2, 19____
Page 1

The use of a contract mining company to mine the (name) Project was evaluated. Quotes were obtained from (name) and (name) late in 19____ . Their estimates were based on profile information from preliminary mine plans and site visits.

To obtain a valid comparison to mining with our employees and equipment, both quotes had to be "equalized." The base prices on a cost-per-ton basis were increased by 7.8%, which included 2.8% for price escalation and 5% for contingency. These same factors were used to modify our base costs in the technical review.

Added to the contract mining base prices was other work requiring the use of heavy equipment that was not specifically included in the stated scope of work. Items that were identified included snow removal, access road maintenance, leach pad ripping, and reclamation (concurrent and postmining). In addition, the technical and supervisory staff that we still would need, to manage a contract mining operation and assaying charges, were added.

The total cost of mining over the mine life, using contractors, ranged from $1.21 per ton for (name) and (name) to $1.26 per ton for (name). The comparable cost for our own mining is $1.19 per ton. Details of this comparison are attached.

Although total mining costs are close when comparing contract mining to in-house mining, there are other considerations. Over the course of the 6-year mine life at (name), the variability of a contract miner's price may be considerable. The prices we were quoted were budget prices only, and did not contain pricing guarantees. An example of the anticipated upward pressure on their prices is wear steel. Although the contractors were aware of the abrasive characteristics of much of the material to be mined, it is doubtful that they cast into their numbers the $0.10 per ton for wear steel that we expect to see and have included in our own direct mailing costs.

Memo analyzing use of outside vendor.

Note: This is a long but clear memo. Its informal style aids the reader's understanding. The memo was single-spaced, but the paragraphs were of reasonable length. Double-spacing and bullets would have allowed easier reading.

One problem typically faced when using contractors is poorer ore control due to higher variability in bench elevations and lower mining selectivity in their loading operations. The result is either increased dilution of ore, which results in higher mining and processing costs, or loss of ore (and ounces) shipped to the waste dump. For example, in (name), the narrow ore structures have caused us to increase mining selectively by use of a backhoe. The contractors propose using front-end loaders, which have more limited capabilities for extracting narrow ore zones.

Finally, it is extremely difficult to quantify all of the projects you would need to perform over mine life. To accomplish these projects, you would have to pay contractors on a change-order basis (they can "nickel and dime you to death" with the added charges). The other alternative is to maintain a small workforce and equipment fleet in-house. Either of these options would add costs to the mining contractor option.

Contract mining has its place in mining, especially for projects with a short duration (under 3 years) and relatively simple ore control requirements. Although part of the (name) Project fits this description (name of example), most of the project would be mined by us. With the cost comparison essentially a wash, the corporation would fully capitalize this project (i.e., buy mine equipment) and mine this project. Alternatively, if we need to limit capital and can stand higher cash costs of production ($260/oz. compared to $219/oz. in this comparison), we should explore further some of the attractive leasing options that exist to mine the (name) Project in-house.

We are, however, continuing to evaluate all options and are in the process of providing (name) an updated package of information on the (name) Project. With this information, (name) should be able to refine the cost estimates. (name) will need to, in a follow-on proposal, commit to long-term contracts that address many more of the facets of open pit mining, offer attractive costs, and provide assurance that (name) will properly mine the orebody, before gaining a future in the (name) Project.

PAYMENTS FROM (NAME) FOR FUEL CLEANUP

Attached please find a check for the amount of $468.56, received today from (name). This is for reimbursement of the mine department's costs in cleaning up a fuel spill caused by one of their employees. My letter to them requesting this reimbursement is attached for your files.

Please apply these credits to the equipment that was used as follows:

223 Loader	$307.40
225 Loader	53.05
243 Dozer	82.14
271 Grader	25.97

If you have any questions, please advise.

Memo on cost of cleanup.

Note: Simple, easy-to-understand internal memo.

SUBJECT: *July 1, 19____ ORE RESERVES*

I have attached a copy of the draft July 1, 19____ , ore reserves statement. The reserves by pit/area were derived as follows:

1. *ECONOMIC—DEMONSTRATED*

Area	Gold Price	Reserves Basis
North Pit	$400	Ultimate pit design using Sep. 19____ MIK model.
Disc Pit	$400	Ultimate pit design using Jan. 19____ MIK model.
South Pit	$400	Ultimate pit design using Aug. 19____ MIK model.

2. *MARGINALLY ECONOMIC*

Area	Gold Price	Reserves Basis
North Pit	$400	Ultimate pit for demonstrated, floating cone using March 19____ MIK model for inferred.
Disc. Pit	$400	Ultimate pit for demonstrated, floating cone using April 19____ MIK model for inferred.
South Pit	$375	Ultimate pit using Sep. 19____ MIK model created by (name).
Section (#)	$460	Mine design using Jan. 19____ MIK model.
West Pit	$400	Floating cone using March 19____ IDS model.
Section (#)	$400	Floating cone using June 19____ IDS model.

I have categorized the reserves based on current economic viability. I will defer to your expertise for these final determinations. If you have any questions, please call.

Memo reporting on reserves.

Note: Clear, well-organized report on reserves, which could be utilized for inventory as well.

June 5, 19____
Page 1

1. *Summary.* Both the (name) and (name) flotation Projects are scheduled to be presented to the Board of Directors on July 27, 19____ for approval. The complexity of these projects due to their interdependence and the need to complete the Technical Review document by July 9, 19____ makes it critical that deadlines outlined in this plan of action are met by anyone listed as an action party. Any delay will affect the overall process and may make it impossible to meet our schedule.

2. *Technical Review Framework.* A meeting was held on April 6, 19__ at (name) request to resolve several questions relating to the processing of (company name) flotation concentrate at (site name). At this meeting many of the questions posed and approaches for completing the project on time were discussed. As some initial choices were made and issues resolved, the elements of the technical review evolved. The results include:

   a) Prepare a single Technical Review document and bring to the board a single project entitled "_____ Project" ("Project"). The "project" economics will compare the incremental advantage of constructing the (name) mine and a 4500 tpd flotation plant to process low grade sulfide ores at _____ . The economic parameters (IRR, NPV, operating and net income, cash flows, etc.) will be derived from the following formula:

   "Project" Economics =

   b) Describe in the technical review the effect of the "project" on last year's long range plan including gold production and production cost details.

   c) Explain in the technical review the allocation decisions that were reached and that the final choices were made to "minimize leakage" due to tax effects. Describe types of

Project update memo.

Note: This lengthy memo on mining projects was preceded by a summary so that management could absorb what was going on without going through the entire report. Responsibilities and due dates are clearly spelled out so there is no confusion.

allocations made and highlight the inter-dependence of _____ and _____ flotation plant.

d) Prepare production and cost details ("Reporting numbers") using the assumptions made in c) for _____ and _____ . This information should be packaged as separate technical review supporting documents for each mine.

e) Defer work on options under consideration that cause slippage of the schedule and preclude completion of the July 9, 19____ Technical Review document. These include consideration of the Section 9 mineralization at _____ and detailed examination of processing alternatives that abandon use of the current _____ autoclave. Work currently underway on the 7000 tpd flotation plant that will generate "go/no go" decision points within the next few weeks should continue on a parallel stream with the base 4500 tpd plant. The overriding consideration remains to get the 4500 tpd plan which has minimal impact on the continuity of _____ operations completed the cast into a technical review on time. Only if the 700 tpd option looks significantly better than the 4500 tpd option, should this approach be altered.

f) Prepare three mine cost models: _____ , _____ with a flotation plant and _____ without a flotation plant. The first and second models will be used to prepare the "Project" economics and production data. The third model will be used to prepare the "base" case.

g) Make the following assumptions for the initial pass at "project" economics:

_____ produces flotation ounces and receives credit for their income.

_____ pays concentrate shipping costs.

_____ pays _____ a processing cost comprised of a pro-rated share of operating and capital costs.

_____ does not mine Section 9.

When _____ runs out of whole ore in
_____ , _____ concentrates are processed
either by an outside company (i.e., _____) or run
along through the _____ autoclave stand-alone
depending on the most favorable costs.

3. *Action Plan.* To achieve the work outlined above will require considerable efforts and coordination. The tasks, person responsible for the task, and due date for their efforts are as follows:

Description of Task	Responsible Person(s) Due Date	
a) Develop templates for economic cost models for "project" and "base" cases.	L. _____	Apr 20
b) Complete mine costs model for _____ without a flotation plant	M. _____	Apr 25
c) Complete mine cost model . for _____ with a flotation plant	M. _____	May 19
d) Complete mine cost model for _____ .	M. _____	May 19
e) Provide preliminary capital and . operating cost data from the draft _____ study for the "project" case	G. _____	Jun 05
f) Update preliminary economic . models with new cost data from mines/_____	L. _____	Jun 08
g) Using _____ study and preliminary economic model, make preliminary transfer pricing decisions.	J. _____ K. _____ L. _____	Jun 12
h) Re-run "project" economic model to optimize tax/depletion situations.	L. _____	Jun 19

i) Finalize transfer pricing decisions.

J. _____ Jun 20

K. _____

L. _____

j) Re-run mine costs models. Summarize mine-site cost/ production data

M. _____ Jun 26

M. _____

k) Finalize economic model for "project."

L. _____ Jun 30

l) Prepare consolidated LRP analysis with emphasis on financing.

L. _____ Jul 05

m) Assemble text for technical review.

W. _____ Jul 05

n) Complete technical review document.

D. _____ Jul 09

In the three years you have been with our company, several things have become obvious to me: You have a work ethic second to none, and your attitude in sharing and helping others is unparalleled. It has been a pleasure having you on our team, and I commend you for a performance that has been consistently outstanding.

My only wish is that our entire department was filled with (name). Thank you for your support . . . and for being here.

Memo complimenting employee on performance.

Note: No note is more valued to an employee than a complimentary memo that can be inserted into their personnel file as well as given to them. Managers sometimes forget the value of these notes.

It is with great pleasure that I inform you that the management committee has unanimously approved your promotion to senior project engineer. Your work ethic, loyalty, diligence, and creativity at our company during the past years is something that everyone, including the management committee, has been cognizant of for a long time.

There is not another person in our group that deserves this promotion more, and I look forward to many more years of working with you.

Congratulations, (first name), for a promotion that is certainly well-deserved.

Memo informing employee of promotion.

Note: A written notification of a promotion by a supervisor adds to the verbal notice that preceded the promotion.

It is with great pleasure that I announce the promotion of (name) to senior project engineer. (First name) has been with us for nearly eight years, and during that time he has distinguished himself and his creative engineering abilities on numerous, key projects. His work on the _____ Unit was not only above and beyond, but it enabled us to garner a contract that we sorely needed.

Throughout this tenure, he has never given less than 100%, and he has made every one of us proud to be associated with him. Join me in congratulating (first name) and wishing him all the best in his new challenges.

Memo announcing promotion of staff member.

Note: A memo giving support and endorsement to a promotion is important because it shows that management is firmly behind the individual.

The _____ Engineering Department needs to add four personnel to adequately support the Production Department in a 24 hours per day, 7 days per week operation. I have attached the rationale and _____ recommendations that fully explain and document their requirements.

The changes will feature one ore control technician rotating with each 12 hour mine crew, 7 days per week coverage by an ore control engineer and a mine geologist. With our ore control considerations with respect to sulfide boundaries becoming increasingly important, we cannot afford to be without full support on the weekends. To do so we run the risk of misplacement of sulfide materials and missed opportunities to reclassify and process apparent sulfide or carbonaceous material through our oxide circuits at a profit.

The surveying department would be staffed to provide two, two man crew coverage, 7 days per week. Too often now we find that because of light weekend coverage we have failed to catch problems in elevation control and in our ongoing construction projects. Work must consequently be re-done at a significant added cost.

In support of this request, I would like approval to immediately post for the following positions:

Description	Classification	Proposed Salary
Ore Control Geologist	Salaried exempt	$_____
Mine Surveyor	Salaried exempt	$_____
Engineering Technician	Salaried non-exempt	$_____
Ore Control Technician	Salaried non-exempt	$_____

In addition, _____ transfers from ore control to the pit effective Monday, April 18th. We have advertised for this opening and have one applicant, _____ who has responded and is qualified. He has served as a temporary employee in the ore control department for several months and I would like to hire him at an initial salary of $_____ /year effective April 16th. Please advise if you have any questions.

Memo requesting approval for additional staff.

Note: Back-up for adding personnel is part of the request.

(Name) just returned from Middletown, and informed me that the (name) Project is running behind because of several engineering problems in the switching station. (Name) did not go into detail, but I thought the three of us should get together and determine what the problem happens to be.

The (name) Project is priority and it would behoove us to ensure that nothing delays its completion. I have asked (name) to set aside next Monday (22), and told him I would check with you to pinpoint a time. Mondays are difficult for most of us, but I thought late afternoon, when the weekend problems were solved, would be the best time. How does 4 P.M. sound? I estimate it will take us about an hour. Would you let me know if that or some other time frame fits into your schedule, and (name) will book the conference room.

Memo requesting meeting.

Note: Meetings usually disturb the work flow and most professionals try to avoid them, however, in this memo the meeting proposer has suggested a specific time of day that may be more palatable to those involved.

Following our meeting this morning on (topic), I had _____ prepare a brief recap and list the responsibilities of those who were in attendance. If you have any questions as to duties and due dates, please see me.

Project	Due Date	Responsible Person(s)
1. Preliminary Plans	12/01/____	J. _____
2. Review of plans/recap	12/10/____	L. _____ /S. _____ /B. _____
3. Costs	01/03/____	H. _____
4. Competitive analysis	01/20/____	L. _____
5. Marketing opportunities	01/31/____	B. _____ /L. _____
6. Proposed production schedule	02/10/____	S. _____
7. Presentation to management	02/20/____	L. _____ /S. _____ /B. _____

Memo recapping meeting and responsibilities.

Note: Spelling out duties and responsibilities avoids confusion, and dates give everyone a definite target.

The pros and cons of introducing our new technology line in April as opposed to July were thoroughly discussed, and the committee agreed to move the launch date to April because of marketing and purchasing considerations.

More specifically, by moving to April we would be ahead of the competition, we would also be able to use all our manufacturing facilities, and the Spring date and its milder weather would be more suitable to the anticipated round the clock production than a period during the summer, since our plants are not air-conditioned.

(Name) will be responsible for plant preparation, (name) ordering the raw materials, and (name) for arranging shipping and arrival dates to distribution centers. Reports from each of the responsible parties are due on January 12.

Memo recapping meeting discussion.

Note: Once again, a memo that clearly spells out duties and responsibilities as well as a timetable.

As is the case each year, our annual audit will begin on (day, date) when auditors from (name of firm) will be here to inspect our inventory. Please be prepared to show the auditors your physical inventory. They will want to count and inspect items to assure that the products listed are on hand and our count is accurate. They may also ask to document our costs.

It is critical that the audit be done in a timely manner, so please be prepared when the audit team arrives. See me if you have any questions.

Memo regarding upcoming audit.

Note: Alerting employees to upcoming events and giving them a timetable is critical for a well-run plant.

August 3, 19____
Page 1

Summary

Primary efforts were focussed on the successful completion of the
technical review document for the "_____ Project" (formerly
called the _____ / _____ Flotation project). This effort
culminated in approval of the project by the Board of Directors on
July 27, 19____ . Other project work this month included developing a
plan for the _____ technical review and updating the economics based on new metallurgical information. Preliminary economics
for the _____ Mine in (State) were also presented at the July
SORT meeting and a data review for the _____ _____
Project was begun.

Flotation Project

The final technical review was completed on July 10th and presented to the Policy Committee of the Board of Directors on the
following day. Their review prompted development of an additional
"what if" case for _____ canyon that looked at the effect
of a 50% increase in reserves. The project was presented to the
entire Board of Directors at their July 27th meeting and was
approved.

Project

Potential reserve additions at _____ this year were discussed
following the monthly status meeting. The main areas where additions
are possible are oxides from Sections 8 and 30, sulfides from the
Pit, and lower grade sulfides in general.

Section 8 is receiving a real drilling push through the end of this
year to tighten up drill spacing for an updated block model. If we are
able to prove up these reserves we may see the addition of 100,000 to

Monthly engineering report.

Note: Every project is covered in a convenient summary leading off the report, and each project is
underlined for reading ease. The language in the report, although prepared by an engineer, is the type
that could be understood by anyone within the company. An excellent boilerplate memo for a project
report.

200,000 ounces depending on how deep the ore can be economically mined. These will still be higher cost reserves if they are added due to depth of overburden.

The Section 30 reserve addition is not likely to exceed 200,000 ounces based on preliminary estimates by geologists. The _____ Pit sulfides have already been modeled and may be included as metallurgical testwork is completed on these ores. Depending on ore grade cutoff for this material, additions of 50,000 to 150,000 ounces may be possible.

Canyon Project

An alternate approach which sites leach pads at the _____ deposit and the _____ deposit, continues to be studied. _____ has completed preliminary site studies for leach pad locations in Section 29 for the _____ Pit. These sites are either too near mineralized ground or would be costly to construct due to terrain or environmental considerations. On the preferred sites, there are currently land ownership issues and costs that will have to be addressed.

_____ *Project*

A schedule outlining tasks and responsibilities for a preliminary technical review by the end of the year was completed and will be reviewed at the August 14th meeting. There will be an intermediate presentation of this information to management in mid-September and to the policy committee later that month to assess the viability of _____ and determine whether to continue to capitalize the project or expense it through exploration budgets.

Other

A review of the _____ mine in Khazakstan was conducted. The company that controls this property is looking for a joint venture partner after _____ pulled out of the joint venture agreement. This is an underground mine which is situated in the middle of one of our large exploration concession areas. They are still pushing _____ , although with _____ gone, this approach is somewhat suspect. The mine as currently proposed is not overly attractive due to high staffing levels and processing concerns. The major attraction, however, is that it is in the heart of our area of interest and it could provide some badly needed infrastructure and local talent to forward our overall efforts in _____ .

The block modeling sub-committee met to prepare an outline for the block model report. Responsibilities were assigned to "flesh out" this outline which will be reviewed by the entire committee on August 15.

A new graphics workstation and a workstation license for the _____ program was approved and has been ordered. It will help us in the underground mine planning for _____ .

Time Allocation

_____ Property	5%	
_____ Property	25%	
_____ Property	5%	
_____ Property	20%	
_____ Property	20%	
Other	25%	

August Projections

1. Responsibilities will be reviewed for the technical review document for _____ , including timetables for accomplishment.
2. Preliminary scoping economics for the _____ project will be prepared.
3. Site visits to _____ and _____ project will be made.
4. A slope stability seminar will be conducted by Chuck _____ in Winnemucca for engineering and operating personnel from all _____ mines.

Recently, our company has become privy to an increasing amount of confidential material, which must be safeguarded. Up until now, our handling of confidential plans has consisted of locking paperwork in the top file drawer of the human resource department. In order to fulfill our contract with the government, we must change this procedure, and offer true security for many of these plans.

Effective Monday, all confidential plans from the government will be locked in a safe on the third floor in Administration. Access to the safe will be restricted, and only those individuals working directly on the project will be allowed to view the paperwork. If any work is removed from the safe, it must be done by two team members, and signed out at the same time.

Security has a copy of this order and will be responsible for maintaining the safe and its integrity.

Memo requesting procedural change.

Note: The first step in safeguarding confidential material is laid out by a department head. Later, more restrictive measures could be instituted and, if so, the memo would follow the same format. Memos of this type should be specific and detailed, leaving no room for misinterpretation.

Attached is an Environmental Assessment Request for an oven that will be relocated from the Detroit plant to the Los Angeles site.

It is requested that a determination be made as to whether or not an Environmental permit is required to install and operate the oven at the Los Angeles site.

If, upon your review, it is determined that an environmental permit is required, please initiate the application process with the _____ so that the planned installation of the oven will not be delayed.

If it is determined that an environmental permit is not required, the City of Los Angeles Building Service Department has been requesting that a letter confirming this fact be obtained from the Air Quality Control District. The City will not issue any building or construction permits without such a letter. It is further requested that a letter be obtained from the Control District confirming the oven's exemption.

If any additional assistance is required, please contact me.

Memo on environmental study.

Note: Moving equipment from one plant to another, and dealing with the government can involve hours of time with regulators. When dealing with regulators—or anyone from the government—it is preferable to always put it in writing. Telephone conversations are frequently forgotten. This memo assures the company personnel that someone from the government has been notified and asked to respond.

Upon reviewing the Acid Recovery Operation on January 9, the following was noted:

1. The automatic acid feed valve leaked through causing level control problems. We suggest a new diaphragm should be installed in the valve.

2. The automatic waste acid dump valve leaks through resulting in the recoverable acid. We suggest a new diaphragm be installed in the valve.

3. All thermocouple wire has gone bad and needs to be replaced.

4. The RTD controlling the acid boiling temperature is several years old, and its accuracy is questionable. A new RTD with a more permanent installation is recommended.

5. The condensate piping on the discharge side of the main steam traps badly. Repiping recommended.

6. The packing in both of the large steam valves leaks badly. Repacking recommended.

7. The access to the valves on the main steam header is now impossible to reach from the Acid Recovery Platform. A platform modification is recommended.

8. There is a hole in the platform around the top of the Tantalum Exchanger. There is also missing decking on the top platform. Handrail also missing. New wood is required for these areas.

9. A larger splash shield is required for the walk way between the recovery unit and the M-Line.

10. Repiping of feed acid and flash steam to the old 17″ exchanger is required for increased operating efficiency.

11. Insulating steam and condensate lines are required for employee safety energy conservation.

12. The gasket on the vacuum ejector has rotted and now leaks. A new gasket is required.

13. The dip pipe water rotameter is cracked and leaking. A new rotameter is required.

Memo regarding equipment review.

Note: Excellent format for inspection of a unit, plant, or other materials. The memo lays out, in easy to read fashion, the problems and solutions.

14. There is a 60 pound pressure drop in the cooling water piping between cooling tower and the acid recovery unit. Due to this loss we are unable to run the heat exchanger at its full potential. Therefore, the recovered acid level is higher than it could be. A new line from the cooling to the acid recovery unit through building 15 is recommended.

15. The iron piping in and around the acid recovery unit is badly rusted and it is suggested that this piping be inspected, replaced where applicable and painted.

16. The gasket for the top of the tails tower has rotted. This resulted in poor pressure control in the separator. A new gasket is recommended.

Waste Water Treatment System

We will be ready to use the _____ Clarifier the week of January 9th. To update the process procedure for the Waste Water Treatment System include the _____ Clarifier and the Flocculator.

Do you have any information on the proper use of this equipment? If not we will have to use "Trial & Error" to determine the proper operating process. One of our biggest questions is when and for how long should the mixer in _____ Clarifier be used?

Please provide us with some guidelines as soon as possible.

Memo requesting operational information.

Note: Situations arise in many departments where new products arrive at a company without complete instructions.

On December 1, _____ of _____ , Inc. conducted sampling for fiberglass and Refrasil fibers during each step of the F10 fiber process that could generate fibers into the workplace. A copy of hygienist's report is attached for your review and comments.

In preparation for the above survey it was noted that a great deal of dust generated during the inspection and handling of the polypropylene bags. In order to control this release of salt particles it is recommended that bags be handled only after wetting with water.

If you have any questions concerning the Survey please call me at extension _____ .

Memo regarding industrial hygiene study.

To: Safety Team #_____ Date: _____ PE No.: _____

From: _____

Subject: Status Report

Congratulations! We have gone another month without an accident.
The winner of the $50 award for January was _____ .

Safety award memo.

Note: This type memo is seen frequently at many plants.

To: _____ Date: _____ PE No.: _____

From: _____ ___

Subject: Spill Cart

During the monthly safety inspection of building (#) on March 8,
19____ , the following items were noted as missing from the spill.

    1 each broom head with handle

    1 each explosion proof flashlight

    4 each organic vapor/acid gas cartridges

    2 bags each _____ safety absorbent

    1 each mop head refill

    1 each squeegee handle

    We also found the spill cart unlocked. With the three additional
full face respirators, the spill cart cabinet is now very cluttered. When
time permits, we need to reorganize the contents of the cart. Also we
need maintenance to add a stiffener to the cart to prevent distortion
of the cart doors when moved over an uneven surface.

Safety inspection memo.

Note: Maintenance was made aware of problems.

Summary:

As per our discussion the following is an outline of Process Engineering's plan to evaluate the Low Tear Strength problem with _____ coated with _____ finish.

Ten drums of _____R62H Finish (old formula) was ordered so that _____ production could resume during the week of 04/17/____ . This product has provided acceptable tear strengths in the past. This production run will be processed under SWR# _____ . Process Engineering will evaluate the first 24 hours of production for acceptability of product tear strength for determination of continued production. All rolls will be sampled after production. Even number rolls will be tested for tear strength, break strength, and % finish for the development of a minimum acceptable tear strength standard. Odd numbered roll samples will be held for retains in case additional testing is required.

Memo outlining problem solving procedure.

Note: Summary gives management background, and idea as to problem and proposed solution.

This memo is a follow-up of our discussion several weeks ago concerning aluminum foil for the Glass Heat Felt. We have found that the 0.005 foil causes wrinkles in the felt that fail the minimum thickness specification. Therefore, we have informed manufacturing not to use the heavy foil. The .001 foil seem to work the best under current process conditions; therefore, order only this thickness for the current GHF production run.

Memo regarding process test.

Note: Internal monitoring frequently requires memos of this type.

To: _____   Date: _____   PE No.: _____
From: _____   CC: _____   and _____
Subject: Betz _____ Polymer

Process Engineering has been evaluating an alternate supplier of polymer for the waste water treatment system. We have now selected a polymer from _____ Chemical Company that provides twice the setting rate at half the concentration. A scale up evaluation drum is currently being ordered. Therefore, do not order any more Betz _____ Polymer.
   Further details to follow.

Change in vendor memo.

Note: Change in vendor and material.

   Process Engineering is providing Manufacturing with a one gallon sample of _____ from _____ Corp. for evaluation as a solvent for cleaning AR and Spanish finish coating equipment. A copy of the MSDS is attached. Initial trials conducted by Process Engineering indicate that this solvent will remove both finishes. The cost of this solvent is $6.15/gal. (1 drum) or $5.49/gal. (2–4 drums) with a $20 deposit on each drum.
   Please review the MSDS and required safety procedures with your employees prior to issuing the evaluation sample. Please note that smoking while using this product is forbidden. Do not use this product on hot steam cans. The use of chemical safety goggles and organic vapor respirator is recommended, especially when cleaning the dip tank.
   If you have any further questions or require alternate evaluation samples, please call me at _____ .

Memo for evaluating new product.

Note: Aside from the product, manufacturing offers a cautionary statement.

Due to a change in our strategic plan, which was implemented in mid-year by our new senior vice president, our division needs to shift funds from one budgetary area to another. With the increased emphasis on telemarketing and customer service, we have hired outside operators and are running Administration at an unanticipated deficit of an additional $4,500 per month. For the remainder of the year, this means we will run a wage deficit of nearly $25,000.

I would like to remove funds from the brochure and merchandising area, which currently has $32,000 in it. I anticipate that expenditures in this area will not top $6,000 for the remainder of the year, which will enable us to "breakeven" with the shift in categories.

Could you advise me as to the steps in this revision.

Memo regarding budget changes.

Note: Department head note asking accounting for guidance.

October 10, 19____
Page 1

Summary: As per your request, I have prepared an estimate of capital and operating cost expenditures for my group for next year. These are classed under the general headings of capital and two types of operating expenses, engineering and acquisition. Acquisition operating expenses are for travel related to exploration and corporate development late stage project reviews.

1. *Capital.* Expenditures to be capitalized relate primarily to computer equipment and related software and training and some minor expenditures for office furnishings. We have pur-chased a _____ workstation and will be receiving it by September. We will want to wait until _____ completes his assessment of this unit before configuring our current PCs to run as satellite terminals. This will likely push this into 19__ before we add this capability. This will require some new equipment as well as upgrades to our current PCs. With the anticipated increase in foreign project work, we are proposing to add a plotter to be able to get hard copies of drill and mine design information much quicker and also an additional lap-top to be able to run MEDS while overseas and during travels. Additional licenses for MEDS and AUTOCAD to make us legal are also planned. Finally, most of my group arrived after most of the offices had been remodeled and new furnishings selected. There are a few minor items we could use.

   a. Computer workstation network. (Includes
      server kit, 4 PC Xterminal cards, associated
      cabling and licensing, UNIX training) $12,000
   b. Existing PC upgrades to run
      MEDS minesight   15,000
   c. Engineering plotter (HP 650 or equiv.)   10,000
   d. Laptop computer (Pentium 120)   8,000
   e. MEDS license (will total 4 for group)   5,000
   f. Commercial software (AUTOCAD,
      quicksurf)   6,000
   g. Office furniture (worktable, bookcases for
      WF, bookcase for CG, JD)   2,000
      Total capital $58,000

Memo on capital and operating budget.

Note: The budget covers everything from training and travel to outside consultants.

2. Operating Expense—Engineering Group. Operating expenses for my group beyond salaries and benefits can be summarized as follows.

a. MEDS training (includes travel expenses) $ 12,000
   General Training (WF) $12,000
   Advanced Gen Training (CG)   2,000
   Advanced Mine Plan (SP, JD)   4,000
   Exportable Minesight Training   4,000
b. Other training (fee, travel expenses) $ 6,000
   20 man days estimate @ $300/day
   _____ Economic Evaluation
   Course
   Geostatistics Course
   Exportable training for mine operations
c. Seminars/conventions (fees, travel expenses) $ 8,000
   40 man days estimated @ $200/day
   SME in Phoenix—July
   MEDS Users Seminar in Tucson—March
   NMC Equipment Show in Las Vegas—
   October
   Northwest Mining Convention—
   December
d. Project related travel $ 52,000
   Domestic (20 man weeks @ $1,400/wk) $28,000
   Foreign (4 man weeks @ $8,000/wk)   32,000
e. Consultants $ 40,000
   Total Operating Expense—Acquisitions $118,000

3. *Operating Expense—Acquisitions.* Although _____ was added to the staff under the budget of the Exploration group for evaluating acquisitions, this work load will likely be spread among the staff. Estimate expenses in this area are as follows:

a. Project related travel $ 39,000
   Domestic (5 man weeks @ $1,400/wk) $ 7,000
   Foreign (4 man weeks @ $8,000/wk)   32,000
b. Consultants $ 20,000
   Total Operating Expense—Acquisitions $ 59,000

If you need any additional information, please advise.

Most of us are aware that sales for the first six months of the year were down 4%, and our division lost $1.2 million during the same period. Although there are signs of recovery, after examining our company-wide performance for the period, senior management has put a new priority in place—cut costs. Effective immediately, we will limit all overtime, and next Monday I would like a list of possible cost-cutting steps from each department.

In putting these together, please keep several things in mind aside from overtime. Any purchases should be defrayed to next year. Please examine your travel plans and pare wherever possible. Our technology investment is another area that we have to examine, and I would like all supervisors to submit proposed technology cuts next week as well.

This is a difficult period for our company, but we have done well in many other trying times. I understand the anxiety that many of you feel, however, we have been asked to cut costs, not employees. And that is good news. We can overcome this temporary setback, and with the help of every employee we can put our division back on a profitable track. I look forward to meeting with you next week and discussing all possible cuts.

Cost-cutting memo to entire department.

Note: No one likes to trim, but this manager has given those within his area the rationale for doing so. The best tactic for getting everyone working as a team to solve the problem. He has not threatened that anyone will be laid off.

New transportation schedules have been developed for the implementation of 12 hour shifts and affect many workers including some of you who have not had a work schedule change. The new schedules are effective as of Monday, April 25, 19____ with the start of day shift.

For the first time since the _____ merger, a comprehensive look at bus ridership was completed. This pointed to the operation of several bus routes with only a few riders and the operation of an excessive number of vans and buses. The new schedules reflect an attempt to make more efficient use of vans and buses and improve the mechanical conditions of the fewer units we run. Fewer units being operated will provide added time for the Transportation crew to repair and maintain important comfort items such as air conditioners and heaters.

Buses will be clearly labelled as to their destination and employees need to make sure they get on the right one. We will use "Juniper" to signify buses that go to the North area administrative building, shops, and mine lineout building. "Pinon" will be used as the label for buses that go to the South area. Most buses will be direct or "Express" routes to one of those two locations. There will be buses and vans that will stop at both areas as part of their route.

We will also run a van in support of our _____ employees who work the 12 hour shifts. This van will service all 4 crews and will be driven by one of the crewmembers. We have 39 _____ employees and 32 work these schedules. This amounts to an average van ridership of 8 employees and makes it cost effective to provide this service.

Administrative and clerical employees now working the 7:30 A.M.–4:00 P.M. day shifts in the Pinon area will change work schedules to a 7:00 A.M.–3:30 P.M. workday and will also be transported to and from work in one bus instead of two vans.

For bus drivers on the 12 hour shifts, we had hoped to be able to provide fresh drivers from employees who would drive on their days off. Understandably, most of us do not desire to "moon-light" on our days off and the response to the bus driver job posting was limited to

Memo regarding transportation needs.

Note: Any changes in workplace procedures should be clearly spelled out.

one employee. We are now examining two options. One is to use non-employees to provide the round trip bus service from town to work and back and we have several candidates already. The second option is one expressed by several of the current 10 hour shift workers who now drive the bus. They feel that they could safely continue to operate buses after working a 12 hour shift. Mine maintenance, lab, and both plants currently use 12 hour crew members as drivers with good results. Likely we will begin the new schedule on Monday with several current drivers and sufficient relief drivers to drive in the event the primary driver is tired. We hope to supplement them with non-employee bus drivers as they can and need to be phased in.

INTERNAL CORRESPONDENCE

Summary

Funds are requested for purchase of new computer equipment and software licensed suitable for mine planning for the consolidated _____ operation.

The planning requirements for the combined operation will exceed the capability of the present PC-based MEDS mine planning system at _____ . The mine planning system at is incompatible and has been under consideration for replacement by GFOC. Expansion of the present PC-based system would be very limiting in its speed and graphics capabilities. The larger block models and increasing demands of the software dictate that the system be upgraded to operate on workstations as it is expanded.

The proposed system is based on _____ workstations, which are also used as the basis for the DISPATCH system from _____ Mining. Any of the mine planning workstations could be used as a backup unit for a DISPATCH computer.

The cost of the proposal project is $180,000. The proposed project includes expenditures for computer workstations peripheral equipment, software, installation assistance, and training. If approved, these expenditures would be made during the period June–August, 19____ .

Existing Situation

Mine planning at _____ is presently accomplished using MEDS software operating on 386 and 486 PC's. Mine planning at _____ is performed using PITS, a software program developed in-house by GFOC, operating on _____ computers.

_____ has proposed switching to MEDS because MEDS is faster and more flexible than PITS. GFOC management has apparently been unreceptive thus far, principally because they also would

Memo proposal.

Note: This memo is a thorough proposal that covers all possibilities, prices them accordingly, and offers a recommendation. The analysis of each system is well done. A convenient summary is included at the beginning for a manager (or CEO) who does not have the time to go through the entire proposal and budget. This is an ideal boilerplate that could be utilized for buying and installing any type of product or service.

have to switch to MEDS at _____ and the corporate office.

_____ is modifying more and more routines in MEDS to utilize the interactive graphics interface, which is more intuitive and productive than batch routines. For example, the new VBM editor allows the user to draw geological zones on the computer screen, rather than plotting hard copy prints and then digitizing the zones. To take full advantage of these interactive graphics capabilities, _____ is encouraging users to upgrade their systems to workstations, which have much greater speed and graphics capabilities than the fastest PC's. The superior graphics and computing power of the workstation make it the computer of choice for using MEDS in the future.

Workstations also allow routine use of more powerful optimization routines. Recent optimization work performed by _____ for _____ has shown the dramatic advantages of using the _____ optimizer rather than the floating cone routine. The only disadvantage of the _____ routine is that it requires much more computing time than the floating cone. For example, run times for most of the floating cone pits were usually 2–3 hours on a 486 PC, whereas the _____ runs typically required 12 hours on the fastest of the _____ workstations. Since the fastest workstation operates about 5 times faster than a PC, the _____ routines would require several days to run on a PC. Therefore, while the _____ optimizer produces much better economic pit designs, the computing time required is perhaps 20 times greater than the floating cone. Given the magnitude of the improvements in the pit economics, it seems prudent to acquire the necessary equipment to be able to reasonably use this improved software.

Workstations will also provide the additional computing power necessary to handle larger block models resulting from consolidating the _____ and _____ models. The file size of the latest block model for section 19 alone is 56.5 Megabytes. When the model is expanded to include the section 18 and 30 reserves, the size of the model will at least double. The chemical model of the same area to be developed as part of the sulfide feasibility effort could be even larger than the gold model. If we continue to use exclusively PC's for mine planning, we will be severely limited by computing power.

Proposed Project

The proposed expenditures include purchase of the computer workstations, peripheral equipment, software, MEDS license upgrades, installation assistance, and training necessary to fully implement a _____ workstation-based mine planning system.

The configuration of the proposed network system is shown on Figure 1. A total of 5 individual workstations are planned for the following functions/groups:

—Long Range Planning   —Grade Control/Geology
—Short Range Planning   —CAD Workstation
—Geological Modeling

In addition, 5 existing PC's would be equipped to operate as auxiliary terminals (X-Terminals), capable of logging onto one of the workstations to perform work that are not graphics intensive. These PC's would also retain their ability to perform as conventional networked PC's running DOS software and would log into the workstation only when desired by the operator. The file server would be equipped with external hard disk modules to provide auxiliary data storage on the network. The server would also be equipped with a 5 Gbyte 8mm tape backup unit, for routine backups.

The estimated costs for the proposed project are shown below:

Item	Quantity	Unit Price		Extended
Sparcstation	1	$25,530		$25,530
Uninterruptible Power	1	5,000		5,000
Sparcstation LX	4	10,500		42,000
Subtotal			$72,530	
Sales tax @ 6.5%			4,714	
Contingency @ 5%			3,750	
Total			$80,994	

Most of these costs are based on written quotations from suppliers. A 5% contingency has been applied to all costs to allow for minor omissions and/or price increases above quoted prices.

Alternatives Considered

The primary alternative considered was to expand and enhance the existing PC based system. Such a system would be more in speed and capability, and would cost only 11% less than the workstation based system proposed, principally because more PC's would be needed.

Although expanding the present PC system would be cheaper, the PC system would be significantly more limited in speed and graphics capability. Thus, mine planning for the expanded operation would be more time-consuming and realistically could not be done as well. The limitations of a PC system would likely become more and more apparent as the software becomes more and more demanding. Therefore, the greater capabilities of the workstation system was felt to justify the additional expenditure.

Another possible alternative, which was judged impractical, is to do nothing and leave the properties on separate planning systems. Although using both systems is unavoidable in the short term, this arrangement is unworkable in the long term for a number of reasons. Since _____ is proprietary to _____ , no programming support will be available. Training personnel to operate both systems would be difficult and expensive. To achieve optimum designs efficiently, the mine planning for the section _____ orebody needs to be performed using one planning system. Since neither of the existing systems is presently capable of doing so, this alternative was eliminated.

After examining the engineering data from the _____ project, a few questions came to mind, which will help me prepare for my senior management report at the end of the month. I have listed each, and would appreciate your prompt assistance.

(1) How old is the system that is being utilized on the project?
(2) What is the downtime of the equipment during the past 90 days?
(3) Has this system been utilized on a project of this type previously? If so, which one? Was it completed on time?
(4) Have estimates been made as to the cost of replacing the system vs. repairing the heads if they should malfunction?
(5) Are there plans that have been made regarding repair or replacement of the system if there is a complete breakdown? Is there an estimate as to how long the system will be down if there is a problem?
(6) Would a new system save time? If so, how much and has there been an analysis done to see if the investment would warrant the production gain?

Memo requesting answers to specific questions.

Note: Getting answers to specific questions before deciding on an expenditure is critical in today's market. Avoid—as this writer did—asking general questions, because the answers may not be definitive enough. Notice how specific the questions in this memo are.

Due to heavy competition in the industry, prices for both our B and A units have dropped $2 per unit since March. Although we were on target for the first three months of the year, overproduction and market flooding by competitors distorted the entire industry by early April. At present levels, our unit sales will exceed our yearly projections by 4%, but our profitability will be down 2% because of pricing pressures.

Raising prices to old levels does not appear to be an option since our units have little to differentiate them from those of our competitors. Our only option may be extended warranties, which would allow us to charge more.

Until management decides upon the option, I would request that the budget committee readjust our yearly goals, and allow us to project new figures for the last six months of the year.

Memo requesting budget adjustment.

Note: A product supervisor runs into problems with costs, a situation that happens frequently in manufacturing. This supervisor, however, does not just ask for more money, he explains his request with facts and asks for an adjustment of his yearly goals. He also gives management a look at the entire year, and offers some ways in which lost monies could possibly be made up.

Within our shipping area, several of our loaders are not being utilized because they seem to be constantly in need of repair. To determine the feasibility of either repairing these loaders or replacing them, I would like maintenance and shipping to supply us with the following information.

(1) How many loaders are used throughout the day?
(2) How many hours (per your log) downtime on a monthly basis per loader?
(3) Are we in need of new loaders? If so, why?
(4) How long is the average loader down for when sent for repairs?
(5) What is the cost of repairs on a yearly basis for the loaders?

If you have questions regarding this form, please call me at extension 343 or Mr. Hurlitz on the night shift at 356.

Memo requesting data on proposed equipment repair.

Note: A foreman trying to get a handle on repairs versus replacement. If the replacement seems feasible, the next step would be to prepare an analysis and proposal for management. This approach can apply to a variety of equipment.

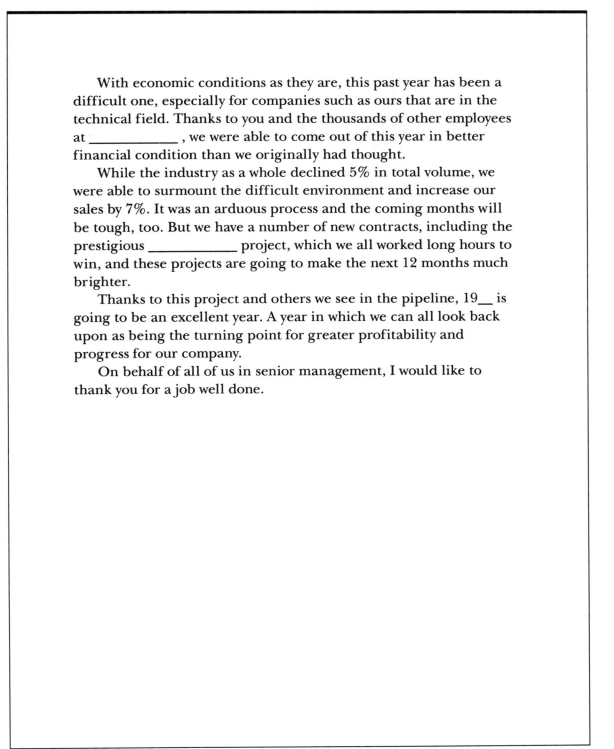

With economic conditions as they are, this past year has been a difficult one, especially for companies such as ours that are in the technical field. Thanks to you and the thousands of other employees at _____ , we were able to come out of this year in better financial condition than we originally had thought.

While the industry as a whole declined 5% in total volume, we were able to surmount the difficult environment and increase our sales by 7%. It was an arduous process and the coming months will be tough, too. But we have a number of new contracts, including the prestigious _____ project, which we all worked long hours to win, and these projects are going to make the next 12 months much brighter.

Thanks to this project and others we see in the pipeline, 19__ is going to be an excellent year. A year in which we can all look back upon as being the turning point for greater profitability and progress for our company.

On behalf of all of us in senior management, I would like to thank you for a job well done.

Memo to employees regarding company performance.

Note: When sending status reports to employees, management does best when it tells the truth. Employees know when times are difficult, and if those facts are hidden, then whatever else management says may not be credible. This is another good boilerplate for a status report.

Since I took over engineering last month, I have discovered that there are several things we should be doing in order to keep closer track on our stored goods and what we are ordering. In the past, each engineer had a separate budget and was able to purchase anything that fit within it. As a result, I have found we have numerous departments with duplicate materials, and we are wasting valuable monies in paying for these.

Therefore, beginning March 1, we are instituting a new purchasing policy. All vendors will deal with one source, purchasing director Mack _____ . Any items needed for your department that are over the minimum authorized amount, must first be approved by the engineering director. Once he signs, the order will be given to Mack, who will negotiate with vendors.

To avoid duplication, Mack is compiling a log of all inventory, both disposable and permanent machinery. It will be his responsibility to notify any department if they order something that is already in stock. If they do, they must be prepared to justify the purchase or share the existing stock item. This procedure will help us preserve cash and will keep our inventory at more palatable levels.

Memo to staff on how procedures are to be changed.

Note: This situation is commonplace, especially in many manufacturing firms where duplicate inventory can exist when more than one person orders. The new vice president is determined to eliminate this dual cost, and he carefully explains his rationale for the change.

_____ Electronics is in need of a company-wide communication system that would tie together the four different locations that are currently in the _____ network. This system must allow for expansion, and for any company that desires to bid on this system there should be a complete analysis of _____ current system, and what the vendor believes is possible.

A complete Request for Proposal (RFP) document is available from _____ purchasing department, and any vendor is eligible to compete for this contract as long as they adhere to the parameters of the RFP.

Deadline for submission is Monday, June 12, 1996, and all must be sealed and stamped by 2 P.M. on that day. The RFP contains details of the submission and requirements.

Memo to contractors and subcontractors for RFP.

Note: RFPs and RFQs (Request for Quotation) are similar, and each has strict rules and guidelines. RFPs and RFQs enable companies that have a multitude of vendors supplying specific products and services, to deal with these providers in a logical, systematic manner. The memo alerts all those on the company's list as to the project.

The Environmental Protection Agency (EPA) is conducting a study on the impact of pesticides in the water supply, and they have asked everyone within our organization to fill out the enclosed study.

Although some of you may not deal with pesticides, the vast majority of us do and are able to answer the queries. You will notice the response is anonymous, which allows each of us to answer questions fully.

I urge you to submit the form as soon as possible, but do not reveal confidential information (such as formulations) in your efforts to assist the agency. Our answers will impact regulations that may be proposed by the EPA.

Cover memo asking recipient to fill out a questionnaire.

Note: Professionals are constantly asked to respond to surveys and it is difficult to get them to do so. An explanation letting the recipient know how the survey will be used will help generate a greater response. People want to know what is going to happen when they fill out surveys.

The long-awaited update on Microsoft has arrived and will be installed by our technicians this weekend.

Unfortunately, there will be downtime associated with the installation, and I am requesting everyone in the company to please be off-line and away from their workstations no later than 3 P.M. Friday, the day before the installation.

If you have a question, contact technical support at extension 785.

Memo regarding installation of new equipment.

Note: A straightforward memo telling everyone what is expected and what they will get.

A few days ago, I E-mailed a request to your department asking if there would be an opportunity for one of your engineers to examine the feasibility of the Marathon contract we are considering. Although technology is marvelous, it sometimes fails and apparently my E-mail was lost in cyberspace.

I've enclosed another copy of the _____ agreement, and wondered if you couid assign it to one of your engineers. Hopefully, this one will arrive. I'll check with you early next week to see if you have received it.

Follow-up memo reminding someone of a request.

Note: A simple request for another department to lend a hand in an analysis. If the request does not come from senior management, the tendency can be to put it aside. The Marathon contract may have been shifted to the side, however, the person asking for the analysis is on top of the issue. Although it is a second request, the person penning the memo remains courteous, a technique that generally gets results.

We are about to install a _____ system at a considerable cost to the company, but before doing so I thought I would check with your unit since (name) told me you had been utilizing a DH since 1992.

If so, there are numerous things I would like to ask before putting our funds on the line. Can you help with the following:

(1) Why did you pick the DH unit?

(2) Has it been dependable? Any breakdowns? How often?

(3) What about its energy efficiency? How does it compare to other units?

(4) What about the service from the company? Are they responsive?

(5) Most important, if you had it to do over again, would you buy another unit?

Obviously, I would be most appreciative if you could E-mail the answers at your earliest convenience.

Memo conducting research on product before using it.

Note: There is nothing like asking a fellow employee about a product or service if they have had experience with it.

Since our reorganization last Friday, there have been numerous questions as to duties and responsibilities, and I am hopeful that this memo will clear them up. I know the memo of Monday, August 7, was confusing, and I think the following will help clear that up as well.

Bob _____ will retain responsibility for quality control. He will report directly to me.

Sylvia _____ will be responsible for our new service excellence initiative as well as handling QC issues that pertain to sinage. For QC items she will report to _____ , and for service excellence issues she will report to me.

Sheryl _____ will maintain responsibility for advertising, and she will report directly to me.

George _____ is new to our department and will be the manager of merchandising. He will report to Sheryl.

I realize there was confusion, especially with Sylvia reporting to two different people, but the initiatives and job functions she handles are in two separate areas. If any of you have any questions, please stop by my office.

Memo regarding staff functions.

Note: A new executive splits duties and tries to make sure everyone knows what they are doing and to whom they report. Sometimes, memos of this type help when there is reshuffling in a department.

Sue, as you know, we are probably going to be faced with cutbacks after the next quarter. None of our engineers know about the status of the _____ project, and the fact it has not gone well and sales are down.

I need to discuss reductions, who would be selected, how, the legal problems and other related problems with you as soon as possible. Could you call and let's set a time.

Memo to human resources regarding staff reduction.

Note: Cutting staff is difficult, and astute supervisors look for guidance from human resources before any mention of cutbacks is made.

During the past three months, our department's volume has gone up 42% when compared to last year. At the same time, our staffing, which was reduced by two positions at the beginning of the year, has remained the same.

The shortage of personnel has impacted us in several ways. Our overtime is up as a percentage of total salaries by 12%. I am also concerned about quality control, an issue that is critically important to our company. With increased volume and less staff, we have not had the time to check each of _____ as thoroughly as we normally do. Consequently, we have seen our rejection rate climb 5% during the past three months.

If we can cut the rejection rate in half and eliminate 5% of the overtime, our department will show a profit increase of an additional 4% by the end of the year. If we took 1.5% of those monies and invested it in one new employee, we would have a net increase of 2.5%, and be producing better products for our clients.

I know this addition to our staff would be of significant benefit to all of us. Could you let me know your thoughts as soon as possible.

Memo requesting additional staff member.

Note: The supervisor of the department needs help, but he backs the request up with hard figures. He shows management the financial and quality difference. Providing specifics will enhance the chances of every request.

19____ was a difficult year in our industry, but thanks to you and your coworkers at the _____ facility, the past 12 months have not only been rewarding, but some of the best in our history. Your performance was not only 20% ahead of last year's, but while the industry was barely maintaining itself, we were way out in front adding business and satisfied clients.

None of this would have been possible without each of you, and I would like to take this opportunity to congratulate our technical staff for the outstanding contribution you made to this firm this year.

Memo thanking all employees for their efforts.

Note: Whether it is a letter or memo, employees like to put something in a portfolio when they have had an outstanding year. Thus, although a one-to-one talk and congratulations is certainly pleasant for the employee, there is nothing like a written document to reinforce the feeling of accomplishment.

"Don't pray when it rains, if you don't pray when the sun is shining." That was advice from the ageless baseball pitcher Satchell Paige, when he was asked about difficult times. The same truism can be utilized in our business. There are always difficult times, but there are good times, too. In the past we have seen those good years.

Now, we are going through some lean times, and I am just as appreciative of these days as when we were doing extremely well. Regardless of the cycle, whether the times are good or bad, our company has an advantage that no other can match: you. The technicians who have given us the best products we can ever hope to manufacture.

It is you who make the difference. So whenever I think of how tough the business is, I think of you and the support, creativity, and knowledge you bring to our company. Thanks to you I know one other thing: it won't be long before the sun is shining once again.

Memo to staff following a difficult time.

Note: This message was sent via memo by a CEO who was in the midst of a difficult sales year. The employees knew about the problems, and morale was sinking. The CEO thought there would be numerous messages he could send, but the one that meant the most would be the one that told employees how special they were.

December 15, marks your fourth anniversary with _____ Industries, and on behalf of the technical staff and senior management, I would like to take this opportunity to congratulate you and thank you for all your efforts.

The strength and growth of our technical division is largely dependent upon individuals with initiative and imagination; individuals such as yourself. All of us at _____ Industries, want to take this opportunity to acknowledge your contribution to our company, and especially for the input and tremendous effort you made with the _____ agreement.

Memo marking an anniversary.

Note: A memo congratulating employees is fairly standard, but if the writer can cite a specific instance—the _____ agreement—then the employee feels that perhaps this is something special.

I need your suggestions and advice on how to handle a delicate situation at the manufacturing facility. Ever since the news of the proposed takeover of our company by _____ appeared in print, there has been a constant flow of rumors filtering down and damaging employee moral. The overwhelming majority of technicians believe that once the takeover happens, there will be massive cutbacks. That belief is widespread, and has grown to such an extent that many of our top engineers have been soliciting, according to rumor, our prime competitors and seeking new positions.

We must do something to stop the flow of misinformation, which is not only destroying moral but putting us behind on many of our key projects, including the _____ initiative.

Any suggestion you might have as to how we kill these rumors and get our employees back to full scale production, would be appreciated.

Memo seeking advice.

Note: Once a rumor starts, employees begin to spend more time discussing it than the job at hand. Memos of this type are frequently found going from production to human resources.

The capabilities of our engineering department have been enhanced with the addition of Janis _____ , an engineer, with more than ten years of aerospace experience. Janis comes to us from (name of previous employer) where she was in charge of the company's highly successful (name of project).

Prior to that, Janis spent four years with (name of company) and was responsible for the production of the _____ aircraft.

Janis joins us next Monday (3). Please stop by and welcome the newest addition to our department.

Memo announcing a new employee.

Note: The welcome and reputation of new employees can be enhanced by citing more than just their degrees. Listing some of the new employee's accomplishments can enhance acceptance by other employees.

Going above and beyond is a phrase that is often spoken, but it is a rarity when we see individuals who actually live it. Jerome, your actions yesterday when Jim _____ had his accident, were clear indications that you are someone who does live it.

Thanks to your timely action, Jim survived a tragic accident and his gratitude, as well as the gratitude from everyone in the company, is something that you will forever have.

I am extremely proud of you, and especially grateful that you are part of our company.

Thank you memo to employee or staff member.

Note: A department head expressing the company's thanks for actions taken. This memo can be modified in many ways. It can express a department head's thanks to an employee who put in extra time and effort, or it can be addressed to an entire department for their efforts.

On behalf of everyone at _____ Industries, I would like to express our thanks and appreciation for completing the _____ Project on time, and with the fewest accidents of any project we have ever turned out at our aerospace _____ facility.

Everyone in the company is praising your department for its professionalism and its accomplishments. Clearly, you have shown what true teamwork is all about, and how important it is to the well-being of a company.

During the past months you have worked on this project, I know all of you have put in countless extra hours and effort to get the job done. In appreciation, and as a special bonus, president _____ has asked that I let each of you know that he and the board have declared next Friday as a special holiday for the company. I hope you enjoy the time off, and thank you for your unparalleled work ethic and accomplishments on the project.

Congratulations memo.

Note: A congratulatory note that includes an award, the day off. There is nothing employees appreciate more than a thank you, especially when it is put in a written format.

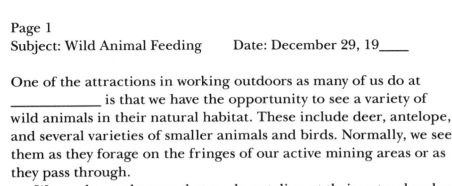

Page 1
Subject: Wild Animal Feeding   Date: December 29, 19____

One of the attractions in working outdoors as many of us do at _____ is that we have the opportunity to see a variety of wild animals in their natural habitat. These include deer, antelope, and several varieties of smaller animals and birds. Normally, we see them as they forage on the fringes of our active mining areas or as they pass through.

   We need to make sure that we do not disrupt their natural cycles and mannerisms any more than necessary. We currently use fencing to try to discourage their entry and have installed waterings outside of our fenceline to reduce the number of animals that might otherwise be attracted to our leach pads and tailings dams.

   We used to have a problem with chukar coming out onto freshly watered haulroads and more than one truck driver has swerved to avoid them. While we may still have this problem from time to time, it was helped somewhat by the installation of a "guzzler" outside the active mining area as well as several cattle watering sites.

   Currently we have a problem with one or more coyotes in that _____ seems to have become their major food source. Originally they were drawn by the leftovers they were able to scavenge out of the landfill area. At least one had decided to eliminate the middle-man and has had a great deal of success begging scraps of food from many of our production employees. He/she has become so bold that it stands within a few feet of trucks, shovels, dozers, and powder crew personnel in hopes of getting some free lunch. This one critter actually runs the circuit of active shovel faces and waste dumps to make sure no possibilities are left unexplored and routinely can be seen staring forlornly up at the operator of a 150 ton truck or some other type of equipment.

   The major concern is that one of us will accidentally run over and kill this animal in the very near future unless we can retrain it to become much more wary of us. There are a couple of secondary concerns in that it is suspected of having chewed on some of our

Memo covering an unusual problem.

Note: Not every company encounters this problem, but the memo is quite interesting.

blasting lines and that it may one day decide to quit begging and attack one of us to get food.

None of us are keen to have this particular animal destroyed; therefore it is imperative that each one of us quit feeding this coyote or any other wild animal. We need to make sure food scraps as well as any of our trash are disposed of in trash receptacles and ultimately in the landfill. Secondly, we need to make sure that these animals do not become so tame that they are unafraid to approach us. Use noise or gestures whenever to chase these animals away from active working areas and let's keep them out of our way to keep them safe.

The Risk Management Workshop which was recently presented to the management group, was a success. _____ did an excellent job of facilitating this topic, and _____ added insight by providing an overview of the scientific relationship to risk management and how the two blend together.

I would like each of the technicians and scientists who attended this session to meet with your team, analyze the ideas that were exchanged during the workshop, and develop an action plan to implement any necessary changes. In 60 days, I would like a report from each of the engineering and scientific teams regarding the following:

1. Did any of your objectives change after the workshop?
2. Did you discover any new opportunities through the process?
3. Did you find any areas that needed control improvement?

For each of the above questions, please provide a brief description of the actions taken or planned. The action report will be used to measure progress toward improving risk management within our experiments.

Your insights and support of this important process are appreciated.

Memo on workshop employees attended.

Note: Management asks for feedback following a workshop that was designed to assess the risks that various departments were taking with scientific experimentation.

Yesterday, I met with Ms. Jane _____ the consultant that the company has retained to assist us in developing a comprehensive service policy for our engineering department.

Ms. _____ , who is a charming and delightful lady, plans to visit the Greeway facility the week of July 18. I had initially intended to be with her, however, I discovered a conflict with an executive board meeting the same day in Arlington. In light of my dilemma, I am turning to you and asking if you could escort Ms. _____ and show her through the facility. No one knows it better. Could you let me know if this meets your schedule, and if it does, I certainly owe you one.

Memo asking a favor.

Note: A congenial memo to a colleague asking a favor. When asking for favors, the more specific—and important—the reasons, the greater the chance the favor will be granted.

Our production has fallen nearly two weeks behind, and we have also exceeded our budget on the _____ project. Of course, none of us started the _____ project with these results in mind, however, we are faced with handling both problems. After consulting with senior management, we agreed to put aside next Thursday and bring the entire technical staff together for a brainstorming session. You are the people who know the project best; and you know the problems.

We will spend the day together, and, hopefully we will be able to develop some solutions that will solve both the budgetary and production problem. The agenda:

1. Overview of project and the initial goals.
2. Current status.
3. Where are the problems and why.
4. How can we remedy them—can they be remedied.
5. Action plan.
6. Monitoring plan.

Memo requesting ideas from staff.

Note: Numerous departments and companies find themselves over budget and under production goals. This company decided to do something before the problem got out of hand. The key elements of the gathering are items 3 and 4. In bringing the staff together, management hopes to find the problem and resolve it.

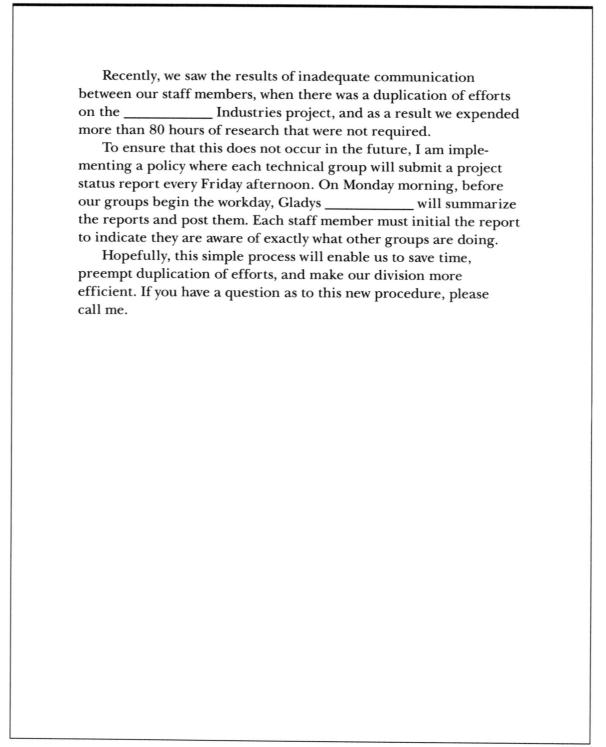

Recently, we saw the results of inadequate communication between our staff members, when there was a duplication of efforts on the _____ Industries project, and as a result we expended more than 80 hours of research that were not required.

To ensure that this does not occur in the future, I am implementing a policy where each technical group will submit a project status report every Friday afternoon. On Monday morning, before our groups begin the workday, Gladys _____ will summarize the reports and post them. Each staff member must initial the report to indicate they are aware of exactly what other groups are doing.

Hopefully, this simple process will enable us to save time, preempt duplication of efforts, and make our division more efficient. If you have a question as to this new procedure, please call me.

Memo resolving problems in staff communications.

Note: The supervisor of a division is aware that part of his team has wasted time by duplicating efforts. The new process is designed to prevent continued mistakes. Events of this type are not rarities and this memo can serve as a boilerplate document for many similar situations.

152

Although your analysis of the _____ paper, had several extremely interesting and perceptive statements, there were a number of issues which I believe you missed, and are of significance.

For example, you quote Mr. _____ , the project engineer in charge, as saying that his equipment "never came up to par for the analysis." Mr. _____ did make that statement, but he also followed on each occasion by saying that "despite this handicap, the results were not skewed in any way."

Mr. _____ also pointed out that the data supplied to his department had been reevaluated four times, and on each occasion there was a 100% match. This hardly warranted your statement that the data "had to be checked four times." It was, of course, gone through four times, but only to ensure accuracy.

Our division certainly appreciates the time you have put into the project, but I feel a more objective analysis would have served us better. I would be happy to clear up any other misconceptions about the results at your convenience.

Memo critical of report.

Note: A project has been unjustly criticized, and the department head answers with a short note that attempts to show senior managers that the analysis was flawed.

With the use of the new fluoride mixture, we have received a query from both OSHA and the EPA for complete analysis, safety precautions, and the risks involved.

To answer these requests, we will need a complete chemical breakdown, any MSDS literature developed, and any experimental data.

OSHA has set Oct. 1 as the deadline for a reply, and although the other agencies have not specified a date, I assume it will not be too much beyond that date. Therefore, we need your immediate cooperation.

Could you send the specifications to our safety engineer by the end of the week. At the same time, if there is anything in the data that would cause concern, would you highlight the section so that we can review it as soon as possible.

To ensure we make the deadlines, we will need your answers by Sept. 10.

Memo regarding the need to check safety procedures.

Note: Requesting data from various departments as part of a safety check should always contain specific dates and requirements.

During this difficult period, I had hoped that we would be able to avoid any layoffs, but unfortunately this is not the case. Aside from the recent contract we lost, there is another that will expire at the end of the month and a third that is questionable insofar as renewal is concerned.

Therefore, I regretfully must inform you that we will be unable to utilize your services after Jan. 6. Your qualities and efforts as an employee were exemplary, and we will miss having you here.

Please accept our best wishes for your future. I sincerely hope it will be much brighter than the past months at _____ .

Employee layoff memo.

Note: Laying off employees can never be pleasant, but it should be honest and forthright. If the layoff must take place, let the employee(s) know why.

It has come to my attention that some departmental members have been consistently late for group meetings and division updates. Although a few minutes does not seem long, it is a reflection of a lack of consideration and teamwork. In order for our company to move ahead in today's highly competitive environment, we need every department to work hand-in-hand with each other; and respect each other.

While tardiness seems to only impact those who are late, in actuality it hurts everyone. One worker late on the production line holds up the entire schedule, throws off our manufacturing goals, makes the finished product late, shipping cannot plan, and our customers do not get their goods when they are promised.

Remember, the impact tardiness has on all of us. Not just you and your department, but the division, the company, its profits, and, of course, our bonuses.

Memo on excessive tardiness.

Note: A senior manager shows how harmful lateness is by pointing out how it impacts the entire company and, ultimately, the bonus of the person who is late.

I've enclosed the materials on the Hudson Project that were submitted by _____ Industries. We will be analyzing the proposal at our monthly staff meeting on the 20th of August, however, due to the length of the content, I thought it wise to distribute it in advance of the meeting.

If you have any questions pertaining to the procedure or meeting, please contact my secretary at extension 897.

Memo preceding proposal analysis meeting.

Note: This memo could be used for any kind of staff meeting; it clearly explains what will happen and what is expected.

Chapter **6**

Boilerplate for Successful Letters

Even the best letter writers have periods of difficulty; a time when writer's block strikes. This boilerplate letter chapter was designed so that anyone, whether they were a skilled writer or not, could tackle any subject and write a clear, concise piece of correspondence in a fraction of the time it would normally take.

Every letter has an introduction, body, and conclusion. Keeping the conclusion in mind will help avoid writer's block.

Aside from the introduction, body, and conclusion format, these letters are written in a style that allows the writer to copy and adapt them for a multitude of purposes. Each letter was selected for its clarity, and its multi-purpose capability.

Please accept my apologies for the mixup that caused you to cancel your order. I, and everyone at our company, are extremely sorry about the misunderstanding and assure you that it will not happen again.

As one of our valued customers, providing you with service excellence is our primary concern. Once again, please accept our apology, and if there is anything further I can do, be sure and let me know.

Letter apologizing for a mistake.

Note: Once the order has been cancelled, the only thing that can be done is to try to save the account.

Thank you for your presentation, our quality control department is already looking into alternative ways of inspecting and clearing the (name of unit). I think the suggestion will enable us to put out a better product and do it faster as well.

Thanks again for your input, and if you have any further thoughts on the project please do not hesitate to let me know.

Letter thanking client for input.

Note: Acknowledging input from a client is an excellent idea, especially if some of that input is going to be utilized.

Your fascinating presentation on "Future Focus" and the direction of the aerospace industry, was extremely interesting and one of the highlights of last week's senior management meeting. All of us gained from your insights on the market, the industry, and where the government is going.

Thank you for a wonderful session, and we look forward to hearing from you again.

Letter of thanks for presentation to board members.

Note: This memo was presented to senior managers by the department head.

I enjoyed lunch, and the discussion we had about the upcoming project. I've enclosed some background material which will help your company understand what we expect from the firm that earns the bid.

Thank you, once again, for lunch and I hope to see you in the near future.

Personal follow-up letter.

Note: The department head sent this as a handwritten note, which is perfectly acceptable—and many times preferable—when you are thanking someone on a personal level.

I thoroughly enjoyed meeting with you and the representatives from your firm, and was impressed by your technology expertise and your knowledge of some of the problems we are facing.

As promised, I have enclosed some material on our system, and what our plan was when we installed it.

If I can assist you in any other way, please let me know.

Letter sent to vendor who has visited the company.

Note: This vendor had visited the company and looked at some of the problems the firm was having with its technology. The vendor is in the process of putting together a proposal, and the information sent serves as additional background.

I enjoyed the opportunity of meeting with you and Steve yesterday, and discussing the various ways we might revise our quality control approach.

As I explained, we are in the process of drafting new procedures, and would be interested in seeing a proposal from your company.

To assist you, I have asked my secretary to send you our original plan under separate cover.

If there are questions I can answer, let me know.

More formal follow-up letter to vendor.

Note: A formal follow-up note to a prospective vendor. Notice there is no commitment, only an opportunity.

Thank you for the lead from (company name), which turned into an excellent prospect and client. They had need for our new data transmission technology, and we were able to reach agreement after only meeting with them once.

We do appreciate your referral, and thank you for thinking of us.

Letter to another company thanking them for a referral.

Note: The writer lets the person doing the referral know how things came out. This note could be handwritten, and there could be a token of appreciation—such as a box of candy—included.

Dear _____ ,

We have completed the clean-up of the diesel fuel spill caused by one of your employees at our mine site on December 12, 19____ . The total cost is $468.56 which is detailed as follows:

8.5 yard loader	4.5 hrs @ $ 68.31/hr	$307.40
12 yard loader	0.5 hrs @ $106.10/hr	53.05
D9L dozer	1.0 hrs @ $ 82.14/hr	82.14
grader	0.5 hrs @ $ 51.94/hr	25.97
Total clean-up costs		$468.56

Please make your check payable to (company name) and mail it attention to me to ensure proper crediting. We understand you have corrected your problem with that particular employee and are encouraged by your response to date regarding this incident.

A report of this incident has been submitted to the cognizant governmental agencies and we hope that our clean-up efforts will be deemed adequate. Be aware, however, that any additional work they may require or any fines that may be imposed will result in additional charges to your company.

I am sure you now have a heightened awareness of the environmental responsibilities involved in mining and we would encourage you to share and periodically review this concern with all of your employees who work at (company name).

Letter to vendor regarding environmental accident.

Note: This letter covers costs and leaves open the possibility that there may be added charges.

Thank you for your inquiry about our service excellence program, and how it can impact the technology and service divisions of (company name).

We have developed these program procedures over a five year period, and believe they could be of enormous benefit to your company.

In the past, we have worked with several organizations in your industry, including (company name). I have included a brochure and some other information about our approach, and look forward to discussing your project in greater depth.

Follow-up letter to potential client company requesting information.

Note: This consulting firm has just sent a note to a prospective client company.

Please accept my apologies for the unpleasant conversation you had with John _____ over the I-Max delivery schedule.

Our company holds every one of our clients in high esteem, and we value the relationship that has been built up between our two firms during the past (length of time).

I have assigned Martin _____ to handle your account, and I think you will find him knowledgeable, courteous and responsive.

If there is anything else I can do, please let me know. I look forward to talking to you again in the near future.

Letter apologizing for the behavior of an employee.

Note: When difficulties between client and company emerge, it is always easy to point the finger at each other, however, the astute way of handling the situation is not to dwell on "who did what" but to remedy the problem.

Four years ago, our company filled the first order ever received from (company name). Since that time the relationship has grown to more than just one of business to business. I think every one of our employees and technicians at (company name) has a special feeling for your company.

The special relationship that has grown between our two companies came to mind the other day when I noticed that next month will be the fourth anniversary of (company name) and your firm doing business together.

It has been a great experience for us, and I hope this relationship will continue to grow and strengthen as the years go on.

Wishing you and everyone at (company name) a happy and prosperous year to come.

Letter of appreciation to a client.

Note: A short letter expressing appreciation for a client's business can be sent anytime, and generally has more impact if it is sent when there is no special occasion.

I enjoyed talking to you (or your agent) the other day, and I have enclosed materials that will give you some additional insight into our organization as well as our Second Annual International Convention.

Our First Annual convention in (name of city) was extremely well received by the more than 1,500 professionals in our group. Part of the excitement was generated by the superb presentation from our keynote speaker (name), and when your name was mentioned as the keynoter for our upcoming Convention there was enormous exhilaration and anticipation.

For our Second Annual Convention in (name of city) we are expecting to double our attendance. I've attached an agenda which outlines the preferred time for your keynote address. If opening day is not convenient, we could move your engagement to the second or third day. We would like to have a 45 minute speech (or 30 minutes with question and answer).

As we discussed, our budget is ($) for the engagement, and if you would prefer we could donate the honorarium—in your name—to a charitable organization of your choosing.

Should you have any question, please call me at (number). Both the members and I look forward to your keynote address. I will call to confirm the arrangements, and see if there is anything else we can supply.

Formal letter to a potential keynote speaker.

Note: A letter confirming a keynoter and giving the speaker several options. Notice the writer is not hesitant to praise the new keynoter and the impact he will have on the gathering.

Thank you for your thoughtful and complimentary letter of Jan. 15 about (name of person), and the prompt, courteous service she gave to you following the purchase of the _____ . It is nice to hear about employees who are going above and beyond, and from a management perspective it helps us enormously when it comes time for incentive compensation and promotions.

Please be assured that (name) and her/his supervisor will hear about your letter of praise. Thank you, too, for purchasing _____ from (company name), and we hope that you will return soon.

Responding to customer's letter commending an employee.

Note: Thank you or complimentary letters received from customers give a company and its managers the opportunity to respond and by doing so they not only acknowledge the customer's praise, but they maintain and strengthen relationships.

I enjoyed our meeting last year at _____ , and always remembered your offer to share information if the need ever arose. Well, frankly, it has. I was recently assigned to handling _____ for _____ , which is a group I have never worked with previously.

I remember from our conversation and the extraordinary knowledge you had, that (name of project) were your specialty. If your offer of assistance still stands, I would like to set aside some time where we could sit down and I could do some "brainpicking" on _____ .

I'd like to discuss this with you in greater depth, and see if your schedule might allow us some discussion time for my new project. The time and place would be at your convenience, of course. I will call to see what you think.

Letter seeking help from co-worker.

Note: Asking for help is not new to any industry. A short note followed by a telephone call will usually bring the two parties together, and most people respond to assisting others, especially when there is some flattery involved.

This letter will confirm our conversation pertaining to the design changes which I requested yesterday (28) for the new conversion unit. The slightly altered bar in the unit enables us to produce a more energy-efficient product, and gives our clients a more reliable unit, too.

I have enclosed drawings and specifications of the new bar. Could you examine the revised unit and let me know if your company can accommodate us; if the revision will cause a delay and how long; and if there is a price differential.

Letter asking for design changes.

Note: New specs require the engineer to request pricing and production information.

Per our conversation of this morning (22), we would like to cancel the order of lugs that were on purchase order number _____ . The order was placed on February 15, and per our agreement, we have five days in which to cancel. During the past few days we have approved a new design that allows us to use 4 lugs per unit instead of 8. With that revised quantity, we have enough supplies for another 90 days, and will not need to reorder until July 1.

If you have any question, please call our purchasing department, and ask for _____ , who has been sent a copy of this letter.

Cancellation of order.

Note: A cancellation made clear with a purchase order number and the reason.

Congratulations on your recent purchase of our Laser II. When you receive the material, it will be in several cartons, and the instructions are numerous. One area that I want to make sure you understand (it is in the instructions as well) relates to the head testing. Please be sure that the head is secured firmly before turning on the test mode. The temptation is to keep the head loose in the event you want to adjust it, however, a loose head with the test mode on can damage the unit.

If you have any question about the installation, please be sure and consult the manual or call our service at 800_____ _____ .

Letter to client who has just purchased complex goods.

Note: Some companies, realizing that purchasers may not follow the exact procedure to operate machinery, send a cautionary letter before the equipment even arrives. The letter usually alerts the buyer of some critically important operational element in the product.

Our legal department has requested us to send the following Non-Payment Notice, which could have an adverse impact on your credit. Our company prefers to avoid legal entanglements and notices, but your invoices are four months old, and there has been no response to a half-dozen letters and notices we have sent.

Before this Non-Payment Notice is entered in Court, I would like to give you the opportunity to contact us about payment, and let me know when it will be forthcoming. If we can arrange a satisfactory payment by March 11, the legal department will vacate the Non-Payment Notice.

I would appreciate a call so we can settle the matter and avoid damaging your credit standing with our firm as well as other suppliers.

Letter asking for funds due.

Note: Payment from this person has been requested on numerous occasions, but there has not been a reply. Thus, this note, which is stern but still leaves the door open for the debtor, is sent.

Thank you for your letter of Feb. 22. Although our technology return department is located here and we took possession of the items, our accounting and refund division is in Denver, and all refunds are issued through that office. An accounting office several thousand miles away may seem awkward, but it has enabled us to consolidate costs and offer our customers lower prices. I have submitted the paperwork and authorized the refund, but it usually takes Denver two to three weeks to issue checks.

I apologize for any inconvenience this procedure may cause. If I can answer any other question, please call.

Letter to customer regarding refund for returned materials.

Note: The company has a good reason for refund delays. Customers understand lower prices, and this firm can offer low prices in part because of the way it handles accounting.

Please accept my apology for any inconvenience that may have been caused to your company because we shipped incorrect design equipment for your exhibit. Although we are still responsible for what we ship, the initial order was placed by someone at your company who, unfortunately, wrote down an incorrect design number.

I have enclosed a copy of the original order, and this afternoon we shipped, via FedEx, the correct design equipment. You should have it in your possession tomorrow morning, in time for the show's set-up. When you return the other design material, we will credit your account.

I hope this has not caused any great problem, and that it does not interfere with the success of what promises to be a great exhibit for your company. If I can be of any further service, please let me know.

Letter recognizing shipment of incorrect order.

Note: The shipping department acknowledges the mistake it made by shipping the wrong part, but it also lets the customer know that it was not entirely to blame. If there is a reason for a mistake, let the customer know. The reason may not placate them but it does show you cared enough to look into the matter.

Per your letter of May 21, we have checked your invoice and discovered that you were correct, our shipping department did send you three 707 fasteners instead of the 727 versions.

The 727 fasteners are on the way to you, and should arrive within the next week. We are also sending separate packing crates and instructions to your shipping department so the 707s can be returned.

I apologize for the error and inconvenience, and thank you for notifying us so promptly.

Letter replying to customer who says company has made a mistake.

Note: Acknowledge when a customer is right. Lengthy explanations are not necessary, just state what you are going to do about the error. The format in this letter is a good basis to use for any merchandise that has been shipped or delivered by mistake.

Your request for a _____ has been turned over to my department. Unfortunately, our firm stopped manufacturing and marketing the _____ three years ago. In its place we came up with another model, the _____ , which operates faster and more efficiently. We have a plan in place where units with the _____ can be traded for the _____ , and a special discount is available.

Although we cannot supply the _____ , (company name) on the Island does carry used units. I'm not sure as to what type warranty they supply, but I do know they have units.

I'm sorry we were not able to fulfill your request, but (company name) may be the solution or, if you decide to purchase a new unit we can be of assistance.

Letter to customer who is requesting a product that is no longer being made.

Note: Even though the product is out of production, the firm tries to help the customer. Providing service is a critical element in the success of any business.

I know you had a great deal to absorb during our meeting, so I thought I would recap the features of the (name of product) and put together some cost comparisons between it and other similar units.

(Name of product) has several distinct advantages over any copier in the same price range:

(1) It is faster. Copies run at 8 per minute. The closest competitor is 6.
(2) Maintenance time. (Name of product) requires checking at 5,000 copies. The competitors require every 4,000.
(3) (Name of product) can use any paper, bond or duplicator. Only two competitors can match it.
(4) Maintenance. Our service department responds in 24 hours or less. Others vary from 24 to 48.

I've also talked to our senior manager, and if you would like to have a (name of product) to try for a few weeks, we would be happy to supply one at no cost. I will call to see if there are any other questions relating to the copier that I can clear up.

Letter to prospect.

Note: This is a good letter pitching the advantages of the copier. Notice the numbered points, which make it easy to read and compare.

I'd like to take just a few moments to express my appreciation to you and your staff for the time you took the other day when I came in to demonstrate our new (product).

Your courtesy and interest were greatly appreciated, and after spending several hours with your staff it is easy to see why your company is number one in the field.

Letter to prospect following demonstration.

Note: These thank-you notes are actually mini-sales calls.

A year ago, I had the pleasure of starting to work with _____ , the research consultant who did such an outstanding job for our unit. Thanks to _____ , we were able to develop a proposal that convinced management our research project would do much more than just spend funds.

Although _____ has spent nearly his entire career on the coast, the other day he told me he was planning to relocate to the midwest. His reasons: his only daughter and her husband were moving there. _____ will be starting from scratch, and will work out of Chicago, but if you need a strategic alliance consultant who has all his ducks in order, _____ is your man.

I took the liberty of giving _____ your name, and explained that I did not know whether your unit needed any outside consulting. If you do, _____ can fill the bill.

If I can tell you anything else about him, let me know.

Letter to colleague recommending or introducing someone.

Note: An endorsement that weighs heavily because the letter writer has had firsthand experience with the consultant.

When President Earl was outlining the qualifications for the Honors Recipient Award, there was one person who came to mind; a person who clearly stood out above all our other colleagues: (name).

Although Professor (name) is relatively new to our campus, his impact has been enormous. From the day he arrived, he has been a team player, as well as someone who has constantly worked to improve our systems and procedures.

Thanks to Dr. _____ , our field laboratory has been revitalized, and we have new and extended hours in which to use it. Our research parameters have been lengthened, thanks once again to Dr. _____ lobbying with the board; and our teaching loads have been lightened, once again, thanks to his skillful presentation that he gave to the Founders when he convinced them of the value of research to the University.

It is clear to me that Dr. _____ is a leading candidate for the Award, and I proudly nominate him.

Nominating someone for an award, prize, or position.

Note: A nomination with clearly stated reasons.

Last week I was informed that our organization had been given a grant to study the impact of high voltage electricity on farm and other rural land. This was exciting news for our group, which has worked hard to obtain the grant for nearly 18 months.

The _____ Institute, however, has split the project into two parts. Initially, they have given us six months to finish our preliminary findings and report on them. If the _____ Board agrees that the study has merit, they will refund the second portion and give us two years to complete it.

This is an extremely important piece of work, and I am convinced it will benefit a good number of our citizens. But, we are starting from ground zero, and we will not be able to complete the first section without assistance. I had hoped that the assistance would come from your firm. I know (company name) has conducted numerous research studies on electrical field impact, with some interesting results. I would like to invite your team to join ours for a project that would be mutually beneficial to all of us.

I will be in (city) next week, and would like to set aside time to talk to you about it. My secretary will call to set a time. I also asked her to send you our research proposal, which will give you an idea of what we are trying to accomplish.

My entire team looks forward to working with you.

Letter inviting one engineer to share a research project.

Note: Benefits without risks.

I am in the process of preparing a study on the impact of hazardous chemicals on western U.S. plant life, and it was brought to my attention that under the auspices of your laboratory a lengthy study on western U.S. plant life was conducted ten years ago.

Although a decade has past, I have read your work and believe there is a great deal of validity that it could add to my summation. Naturally, anything we quote from your study would be credited, and if I utilize more than two pages from your study, there would be credit up front.

As is the case with most authors, I am on a deadline for my grant and I have gathered nearly all the material I need. Your input, however, is extremely important and I do not want to submit my report without it.

I have another 35 days (until June 18) until the complete report is due to the University of (name). I would like to study your results and the raw data during the next few weeks. I will call you the week of May 10 to see if we can get together.

I hope we can put our data to a mutually beneficial use, and I know it will benefit society if we can.

Letter requesting data for study.

Note: Credit will be shared.

The CES was recently made privy to a study conducted by the Engineering Society in which the impact of statistics was correlated with the psychological behavior of those exposed to the results. Although there were many good points made in the study, and Professor (name) validated a good portion of it with blind and controlled elements, the conclusions appear to be preconceived.

The CES board spent an entire day studying the outcome of the study, and we unanimously agreed that there needed to be additional controlled data entered before the study and conclusion could be deemed valid.

Still, we thought the preliminary results were of interest, and you will find them enclosed. Your comments can be made to the ES, with a cc: to CES.

Letter and memo to membership of organization in which comments are made on study.

Note: Not everyone agrees with studies, not even scientific ones. This organization is questioning the validity of a study.

For the first time in our society's history, we are going to be holding a two-day symposium built around three unusual topics: the outlook for engineering, the aerospace connection and the new entrant in the field, the female. We expect this to be the best attended event in the CSS history, and are hopeful that you are able to attend and participate in one of the panel sessions: "Is there life for engineering after aerospace."

As you can see by the provocative title, we are seeking panelists who are outspoken and not afraid to air their thoughts. The panel will consist of five engineers from three different fields, but all with aerospace background. They will each have five minutes to address the topic, and then the stage will be turned over to a moderator who will take questions from the audience for another 20 minutes.

It will be intense but highly informative. We have it scheduled for the first day of the conference (July 9), at 6 P.M. in Stratford Hall. Dinner will follow at 8 P.M., so there will be additional time to answer questions and air views.

We are hopeful that you will be able to attend and participate since this has always been one of your major areas of concern. I will be out of town next week, but I have asked my assistant to call your office for your schedule.

I, and everyone in the organization, look forward to your participation.

Letter inviting fellow professional to seminar.

Note: Informal letter used when the parties know each other.

As you may know, our campus has undergone a complete transformation during the past decade and undergraduates in our engineering classes are now 50% men and 50% women.

For some of our students, this ratio has created anxiety, and they (males, obviously) wonder if there are going to be openings for them when the masses of women hit the market and start searching for positions.

Consequently, the future of engineering, and especially the role that women will play in it, is a topic we have had enormous interest in from our students. In fact, next quarter, during our Spring break (March 16–24) we are having a conference devoted exclusively to "women in engineering and other technical professions." We expect attendees from throughout North America, and would be honored if you would consider addressing the gathering as our keynoter.

Your experience and pioneering in the field are well-known to every one of our students, and your name would certainly be a prestigious addition to the forum. The keynote address would be given on Sunday, March 16, at 4 P.M. in the afternoon, at Founder's Auditorium. It would last around 45 minutes, and there should be 10–15 minutes for questions and answers.

The topic would, of course, be one of your choosing, however, the female entry into engineering and the future of our profession from the viewpoint of a visionary such as you, would be a topic everyone would love to hear.

I will call your office next week to see if we might match the engagement with your free time. Thank you for your consideration.

Letter to engineers inviting them to seminar.

Note: Invitations should always contain details of the events—when, where, and how long.

Although it has been more than six months since I heard your talk, the points you made about cyberspace and engineering left me with an insatiable curiosity. I know you are extremely busy, however, my company would like to contract for an hour or two of your consulting time.

We have opened several retail outlets, and plan to add a half-dozen in the next year, but I am concerned as to our direction, particularly after hearing your remarks.

I checked with your office and they mentioned you get into Denver several times a year. I would like to plan for you to spend some time at our facility during your next Colorado trip.

I will contact your office next week to see if we can arrange a mutually convenient date. To give you an idea of our plans and where we intend to go, I have enclosed a corporate capabilities brochure.

Letter seeking assistance from a consultant.

Recently we opened a state-of-the-art electronics outlet in the heart of our city. Our material includes everything from two way, touch screen video applications to "Internet" and World Wide Web start-up kits.

Despite this variety of goods, we have been relatively unsuccessful in drawing people into our store on a regular basis. It seems we only draw the extremely high-tech people, but our ultimate goal is to draw the masses.

Knowing that you have provided some of the finest consulting advice to such chains as Cine-X and the Electron Shop, I wondered if you would be able to give our company some consulting time as well. We are extremely anxious to explore the areas we are missing and determine why we are not drawing the masses to our new concept facility.

For the next two months, our business will drop and then with the holidays it will pick up. I would like to get you into our shop within the next three to four weeks so we can prepare for the season.

Could you advise me as to your schedule, and who we should call to firm a day and date, and what fees you would expect.

Letter seeking advice from an expert.

Note: Engineering and technical consultants are two of the busiest occupations today, due primarily to the vast numbers of technical people who have opened facilities but do not have marketing expertise.

While attending the CES exposition, I was invited to hear your program on "space and the hidden agenda," a fascinating exploration into what information technology may mean to the engineering profession in the next five years.

Your presentation was superb, and one that would enlighten, inform, and entertain everyone at our CES chapter. I realize you have a busy schedule, however, our next meeting will be on the 24th of March, two months from now, and your presence as our keynoter would be something that every one of our members would enjoy tremendously.

Our function that evening will be special. Normally, we have a business meeting and that is followed by a keynoter. However, this is our annual new member indoctrination, and the business portion of the event will not be held. Instead, we plan to have cocktails and dinner, starting at 6 P.M., with our guest speaker on stage at 8 P.M.

If you are available the night of the 24th we would be extremely grateful if you would consent to addressing our membership. The talk could be 20–30 minutes, with 10 minutes or so for questions and answers. The address you gave at CES would be perfect.

I will be out of town until next Monday, however, I will call you then to see if your schedule is open.

We're looking forward to your talk, which will unquestionably be the highlight of our year and will certainly give every engineer insight into our profession and what we can look forward to in the 21st Century.

Letter soliciting a guest speaker or presenter.

Note: A request should display knowledge of what the speaker has to offer.

Per our conversation that we had this afternoon, we recently purchased a complete, dual drive Chestnut System, but due to unanticipated growth in our production unit, we need to increase the capacity of the System without losing quality control.

Could you send us a specification sheet on the Duvalier System, and any information you have about its capability with the Chestnut. Are there problems in joining the two? Any previous history?

Our chief engineer, (name), is out of town presently, but he is due back next week. I anticipate (name) will be calling your firm, and going into the specs in greater depth. Before he arrives, however, it would be of significant benefit if we could have the requested information on the Duvalier.

Letter regarding replacement of a product.

Note: This firm bought a piece of equipment and then discovered that it had already outgrown the capacity of the machinery. Before jumping into the first solution that comes along, this manufacturing vice president has started to survey a variety of options.

We are in the process of evaluating several new systems that will require extensive use of pipes, fittings and valves. Our specifications clearly spell out what we need, and I have enclosed one for your perusal. Our goal is to make a decision within the next 30 days, install a test system with 60 and begin full installation within 120 days.

Our project engineer is (name), and he will be calling you shortly to discuss the possibilities of your system as our replacement. Mr. _____ will have all the technical data, and he will need complete pricing, scheduling and an idea of the amount of training you would be providing to our staff engineers.

Letter requesting specifications or information on new equipment.

Note: Pinpointing the proper replacement systems is difficult. Most companies have a set specification sheet, which is forward to a proposed supplier.

Mr. _____ , who was formerly employed by your company between Jan., 1991 and Feb., 1995, has applied for a structural engineering position with our company. We are considering hiring (name), and would like verification of employment for those dates, and any other pertinent data you might have.

Mr. _____ also listed (name), your engineering vice president, as a personal reference. We have tried to reach (name), but have not been able to talk to him. Could you help us by passing on whatever information human resources has on Mr. _____ , and seeing if (name) might be available to talk to us (via telephone) as well.

Thank you for your prompt attention in this matter. I'll call you next week to see if I can provide any additional information.

Letter requesting an employee reference from another company.

Note: Human resource departments are limited in what they can say about an employee, and the above letter is cognizant of that difficulty. The writer leaves the door open by asking the human resource supervisor for "whatever information it has on Mr. _____ ."

I recently returned from our storage facility and found a number of the products your company has produced for us are changing coloration. Although this may not be a serious problem at present, I am concerned about the long term impact on the quality of the units.

I would like to meet with you, (name), our mechanical engineering chief, and (name), our plant superintendent, at your earliest convenience. The three of us have left next Monday and Tuesday open, if that is convenient. I would like to investigate the issue and settle it as soon as possible since we will be moving a number of the products to another facility next month.

Could you call my secretary at extension _____ and let her know your availability. Thank you for your assistance.

Letter requesting meeting.

Note: Asking for a meeting is one thing, but pinning down the day is equally important. If the meeting is going to be difficult, many people may try to steer clear of it. However, if the day is named postponing the issue becomes more difficult. Always try to be specific, especially when it comes to resolving a problem.

In a recent poll of our membership, "future communication—the unusual new vehicles," was voted to be the number one topic that those within our group would like to hear about. Needless to say, as the most prominent speaker on the subject in the country, your name was on the top of everyone's selection ballot, and you were the number one choice to be the keynoter at our quarterly meeting August 6.

The meeting, which will be held at the (name place), will be attended by the top communicators in our industry, and the entire Conference will be themed around "future communication." I think you will find the Conference and our members to be an enthusiastic, stimulating group with an array of intriguing questions for you.

Our keynote address will be given at 9 A.M. on the 6th, and we expect more than 300 to attend. Generally, our keynoter talks for approximately 30 minutes, and answers questions for another 10–15. Those parameters can be adjusted, however.

Thank you for your time and consideration, and we look forward to your August presentation.

Invitation to someone to give a speech.

Note: This letter involves significant flattery—which usually helps when requesting anything.

Dear _____ ,

Your generous contribution of time and interesting presentation of Manned Space Flight Awareness information to our employees on March 6 was greatly appreciated. You repeated your presentation three times from 2 P.M. to 5 P.M. on that day which enabled 52 of our employees to attend. Your contribution has been obvious judging from the enthusiasm and interest in the handouts and gift catalog. Our employees are now relating to their important contribution of producing, testing, and shipping carbon fabric for the booster rocket motor exit cones. You've been instrumental in motivating our employees to do their very best in producing quality materials to meet and exceed our customer's expectations.

Thank you, once again (name), for an enjoyable, informative message from (company name). I'm positive that both of our companies will share in the benefits from this effort to educate and reward our most valuable resource—our people!

Letter thanking speaker.

Note: Good, informal thank-you note.

Dear _____ ,

The 10th anniversary issue of *Best of Business* was forwarded to me from my previous office and since receiving it, I have carried it in my briefcase to read at every opportunity. It is coffee-stained and dog-eared from sharing this issue with my business associates. We agree that it is one of the best collections of interesting, informative, provocative, and entertaining business articles published in years. Our compliments to the editors and all those talented writers who contributed to this issue.

Letter complimenting publication.

Note: A similar approach can be used for speakers.

I recently read your article on the Internet that appeared in *PC News*, and found it fascinating, extremely knowledgeable and informative, and something that every one of our members in the (American Engineering Society) AES would find equally as desirable. Because of the article's implications and the possible impact on our membership, I would like to request your permission to reprint it in our January, 1996, newsletter, which will go to nearly 35,000 members.

Our newsletter (I have enclosed a copy) is geared solely for the professional, and every one of them is intimately involved in information technology. Our January issue will be devoted solely to the Internet and the outlook for its future. We would not be distributing the article beyond the membership. I have enclosed a permission slip, along with a stamped, self-addressed envelope for your convenience.

If you could return the slip as soon as possible, we would all be most appreciative. If there is some problem with reprinting rights, could you let me know as well.

We look forward to seeing (name of article) in our January issue.

Letter asking permission to quote.

Note: Asking for permission requires that there be a permission slip. The person requesting permission clearly explains how the reprint will be used, who will get it, the limitations, and why they would be interested in reading it.

Dear _____ ,

This letter is confirming our intent to purchase a hydraulic shovel and nine (9) haul trucks from (company name) contingent on the following:

   1) An October 17, 19____ approval of our sulfide project from our board of directors;

   2) Delivery of 6 of 9 haul trucks (barefoot) on or before February 29, 19____ with the remaining 3 to be delivered no later than March 31, 19____ ;

   3) Agreement on options availability and pricing; and

   4) All payments for equipment deferred until January, 19____ .

   If these terms are agreeable please sign and return one copy of this letter.

   Thank you, we find these terms agreeable.

_____
(name of company signing)

Sincerely,

(your name)
(your company name)

Letter as purchase order.

Note: When buying anything, companies need to be specific.

Our staff went through your weekly progress report, and although we are pleased with most of the project, we are concerned about several items that were not covered in depth. Last month, your firm reported that it would not be possible to complete the pad by the specified date in the contract. Although we expressed the disturbing nature of this problem, we have not received any further information on the status of the pad.

A second item that has us wondering is the support for the pad. Your preliminary reports that were issued four weeks ago on March 3, indicated there could be a weight issue. We have not seen any further information concerning this aspect of the project, either.

Next week, I will be out of town, however, I am extremely anxious to get these issues resolved and report the findings to our group. I will be back on April 16, and would appreciate a call from your office to bring me up to date on both items.

Letter expressing concern over progress of project in progress.

Note: A business-like tone from a company that is obviously concerned about certain aspects of a project. Notice the note is formal, and lists specific dates for follow-up. When a project is running behind or encountering difficulties, specifying dates is a must.

We have examined your preliminary plans for Project (name), and found them to be right on track with two exceptions. First, the approach to the wind tunnel should be wider if we are to have enough room to get the model inside. An examination of the diameter and width concerned all of us as the model may not be of the exact specifications which you found on the initial plan.

Second, there was concern about the mount and its ability to withstand the added weight of the processor. The opinion of our engineering group, was that the mount's supports should be strengthened. Although no exact increase was specified, engineering would like to address this issue in a conference call on June 6, at 10 A.M., if that date and time is convenient.

We were extremely pleased with the progress of the project. You are right on schedule, perhaps even a few days ahead, and that is one aspect of the job that everyone here and in management certainly appreciates.

Please advise me as to the feasibility of the June 6 call, and if you and your staff would be available.

Letter for project in process.

Note: The contracting engineering company issues a progress report complimenting the subcontractor, but also bringing up several areas of the project that need to be revised. The tone of the letter is informal. The informality makes the recipient feel much more at ease, and does not turn the two difficulties with the project into a crisis.

When we discussed the _____ the other day, I led you to believe that our deadline would be sometime in mid-August. Since that time, however, our strategic plan has been reorganized and the _____ has become a key strategy in our 1996 plan. Obviously, with management putting a priority on this area, I need your plan by the first of August.

I know this is probably an inconvenience, but if you could it would be greatly appreciated by some clients who will be in your debt. Please give me a call after you have a chance to evaluate the work and the new deadline so we can discuss it in greater depth.

Letter requesting elimination of time extension.

Note: Usually outside vendors ask for additional time, however, this time it is the company asking the supplier to move up the delivery date. If a contract exists the supplier may not have to oblige the client.

Due to difficulties within our analysis laboratory, I am requesting an additional five days on the _____ Project, and estimate we will have the final results to your department no later than Friday, Dec. 6.

Originally, I had promised that our firm could do the entire project within 30 days, however, we have had a series of misfortunes impacting our lab—from ill employees to damaged deliveries from suppliers on some of our materials.

I hope the additional five days is agreeable. I'll call you later this week to see what your thoughts are on the added time. Please accept my—and my company's apology—for any inconvenience we may cause _____ Industries.

Letter requesting time extension.

Note: A delay is asked for, but the project supervisor explains why it is needed.

As you know, we have had a local trucking strike for the past two weeks that has hindered our deliveries and caused us to run anywhere from ten days to two weeks late on our new computer orders.

Fortunately, the strike has been settled and we are back on schedule. Your new unit is scheduled for delivery on the 14th.

Letter explaining delayed delivery.

Note: The letter explains the delay, however, it could be more impactful on the customer if there was an apology.

Please accept my apologies for the problems you have had during the past two months with our receptor unit. I have studied our repair records and apparently the problems with the unit started with installation. I have asked (name), our chief field inspector, to call you immediately, set up a convenient time for him to visit the site, and determine exactly what the problem happens to be.

(Name) is an exceptional technician, and I feel confident that he will resolve the problem, or replace the unit, within the next few days.

I realize that the malfunction of the unit has caused your firm considerable problems, and I apologize, once again. If we can be of any further service, please let me know. I will be talking to (name) daily, and will keep abreast of the progress he is making.

Letter to resolve a complaint.

Note: Service problems can cause considerable damage to a company's reputation. The rapid manner in which this firm responded was admirable.

We made a mistake! And we admit it. When your complaint was entered on July 15, it should have gone through our processing department the same day, and a technician should have been calling you to set an appointment at your plant within hours.

That did not happen. We had a computer breakdown, which is usually construed as a manual problem, that erased any complaints we received that day. With our system there was no way to capture your complaint. It was lost and we did not receive additional word until you submitted your second complaint this morning.

Please accept my apology for the delay. You should be receiving a call from our technician tomorrow afternoon, and the problem should be remedied by the following day. If there is anything additional I can help with, please let me know.

Once again, I apologize for losing the paperwork.

Letter responding to service complaint.

Note: Admitting you did something wrong usually improves the situation. People respect honesty, and although this manufacturer was somewhat disturbed, they understood what had happened. This letter was also sent FedEx to show the concern of the company.

This will acknowledge receipt of your letter dated January 14, concerning the problems you have experienced with our new Board. Please accept my apologies for any inconvenience the unit has caused. Immediately upon receipt of your complaint, we started looking into the problem.

After countless hours of engineering time, we have discovered that the trouble stems from a faulty switch, which our subcontractor inadvertently installed in all our "B" Boards. In addition to your Board, we are in the process of making similar changes in every client's product.

I'm extremely pleased that you notified us. As you can see, your assistance enabled us to head off a great many potential problems. As a token of our appreciation for your assistance, I have taken the liberty of enclosing a gift certificate.

I have asked our field representative, (name), to personally deliver your revamped Board and install it. He should be in your plant no later than next Wednesday. Hopefully this will resolve the problem. If you have any further concerns, please feel free to contact me directly.

Letter answering a complaint letter.

Note: A gift certificate is a nice touch. The amount is not important, the gesture shows that the firm appreciates the customer.

I'm extremely pleased to announce that (name), formerly of _____ company, has joined our firm and will be in charge of our west coast technical support department.

The addition of (first name) gives us the expertise that we have always wanted in the technical area. His past accomplishments are certainly significant. For those of you not familiar with (first name), he spent four years with (company) as director of technical support.

(First name) is an innovative, creative individual, who is anxious to meet you to ensure that your needs are being met by our support staff. Sometime during the next month, (name) will be calling to set up a time when he and representatives from your company can get together to mutually explore ways in which our technical support department can better serve you.

Letter to clients telling them about improved service.

Note: The addition of a new employee gives a company the opportunity to contact clients and announce their new expertise.

I hope you understand that my writing to you is solely in the spirit of friendship about something that came to my attention a short time ago, and has me concerned.

Our accounting department has told me that payments on your invoices have been later each month, and that you now have balances as old as (days). My initial thought was that, perhaps, this was just an oversight on the part of your payable's department. When we entered into our credit arrangement, certain terms were spelled out which we both agreed to honor. I think it is important for both of us to continue to follow those terms.

If there is a problem that I am not aware of, please let me know. We are grateful for your business and anxious for our relationship to continue. Please call if I can be of assistance.

Letter seeking payment on a past due account.

Note: This letter seeks payment, but does not insult a valued client. At the same time, the note gives the client an opportunity to call and explain any problems that might be occurring.

Dear _____ ,

    We live in a fast-paced world and our bills and obligations frequently take a back seat to other problems. I know that is what probably happened in your company's situation.

    Our accounting department informed me that you were overdue on three invoices. I asked them to hold up on sending the standard "past due" notices, since your company has been a valued client for a number of years. I felt that any letter regarding past due bills should come from my office, not accounting, in view of our friendship over the years.

    We have, I believe, built a solid relationship between our companies and I sincerely want to keep it. Could you give me a call this week so we can discuss the past due billings, and any problems that you feel we are not aware of at this time.

Letter requesting payment on a past due account.

Note: This letter definitely asks for money, but does so in a friendly tone.

From your past correspondence and the telephone talks we have had, I know your company has been delighted with our equipment, however, we have two new models coming out in late June that I thought you would want to know about.

Our brochures are not printed, as yet, but I had copies made of the page proofs. Although it is not bound, you can get a good idea of how improved the system is and what it could mean in increased production.

Our field rep, (name), is going to be in your area next month, and I suggested that he might give you a call. (First name), will have the specs and further details on the product.

If I can supply any other information, please let me know.

Letter notifying existing clients of a new product that is coming to market.

Note: The home office has opened the door for a field rep to present a new product to a customer.

Thank you for submitting the initial plans for the ramp to my office last week. We have gone through the requirements, your comments as to the unforeseen factors that could impact the ramp, and your suggested structural approach. We agree with your assessment, and the committee is authorizing you to continue the project as you have outlined.

Completion date remains July 12. If you have any problem with this date, please notify my office as soon as possible.

Thank you, once again, for the prompt submission.

Project status reply letter to vendor.

Note: This letter acknowledges that plans are progressing as hoped, but the company is leaving the door open for the contractor to express any problems.

Dear _____ ,

Thank you for your patience with the (name) project. Your submissions were timely, and certainly met our deadlines, however, we have been having some procedural problems within the company and our purchasing department. Despite the delay, and the lack of decisions as to your proposal, we definitely want you to go ahead on the remainder of the project as you initially laid out in your plan of Sept. 5.

If my understanding is correct, proceeding on the remainder of the project will not be a problem, even though we are holding on phase I. I hope to supply you with an answer to phase I no later than next Friday (Nov. 8). However, we would like you to go full-speed on the remainder of the project in the meantime. We still have our overall deadline of Jan. 7 in place, and your continuing on the remainder of the job will ensure that we make our completion date.

If you have not heard from me on phase I by next Wednesday (Nov. 6), please call my office and we will try and get the matter resolved.

Letter to vendor waiting for reply on proposed next steps.

Note: This is a letter from a company that is having an internal problem approving a portion of a project. The company does not want to delay the project, so it authorizes the vendor to proceed.

Thank you for your interest in our product line. I've enclosed a new catalogue which includes the technology applications you were interested in seeing.

Our firm has been in the field for (number of years), and we have developed an expertise in a wide number of approaches to mechanical production facilities. I would be happy to provide additional information, or have our field engineer, (name), contact you at your convenience. Mr. _____ can be reached at (505) _____ _____ .

Or, if I can be of any further service, please give me a call.

Letter answering product inquiry.

Note: This letter could be improved by a more aggressive follow-up stating that "he would call" to see if he could be of any additional assistance.

I was extremely interested in hearing about the software needs your company has during the (name) trade show last week. Unfortunately, with the tremendous amount of people coming through we did not get a chance to spend more time together. I have taken the liberty of putting together a package on our new Phase II software, which will give you an idea of its capabilities and how it ties into your present system.

(Name), our midwest representative, will be contacting you in the next week or so to see if there are any questions that he might answer. Or, if I can be of any additional assistance, please call.

Letter to prospect who visited engineering booth at trade show.

Note: The engineer has opened the door for the rep, and has given the prospect the opportunity to deal directly with the parent company. Shoveling a prospect off to a rep is not always the best tactic.

Dear _____ :

We have just completed the second round of computer training that we arranged through (name) and are generally pleased with the responses we received from our attenders. A notable exception is the DOS/Windows class which was conducted on Tuesday, July 26th. Your instructor for this session was (name). Reports I received regarding her instruction were resoundingly negative. Major criticisms included poor organization, lack of patience with some of the less knowledgeable, and lack of direction particularly in the afternoon session. For most of the attenders it was a waste of their time and for (name of company) it was a waste of our training dollars.

Contrasting this poor performance was that of (name) who instructed the remainder of the three day series. She is an excellent instructor and provided us the professionalism we expect for a college-level instructor.

We have in the past sent our people to (name) and beyond for this type of training and unless we have assurances from you that we will receive a high level of instruction, we may be forced to resume this practice. This would be unfortunate as (company name) has committed to support the college and you are ideally situated to provide us more cost-effective training in these areas.

I look forward to your attention to this matter.

Letter criticizing training.

Note: This letter gives the instructor's name along with specifics.

Ref: No. PE: _____

Att'n: _____

    The following summarizes your request for a written description of the source of volatile and semi-volatile organics in (company name) waste water filter cake, tentatively identified by (name) Associates on Lab Report No. _____ , March 7, 19____ . The primary source of these organics is from the finish on our fiberglass precursor. During processing the fabric is washed and a portion of the finish is removed. The waste water from this operation enters our waste water treatment system where the suspended solids are removed in the form of filter cake. It is assumed the remainder of the organics detected may be from accidental release of oil and grease used in lubricating our processing equipment.

    If you have any other questions please call me at (213) _____ _____ , Ext. _____ . A copy of the lab analysis in question is attached.

Letter reporting study.

Note: This format can be used to analyze and report on other materials.

Dear Sir:

      _____ Materials Division, is a Generator of hazardous waste. We are not a treatment, storage disposal, or recycling facility. Therefore, we are not required to complete the Facility Hazardous Waste Report for 19____ The Department of Health Services granted us a variance in 19____ for our elementary neutralization system. See attached copy of variance. It is our understanding that this letter will be accepted as the requested affidavit certifying that our site is not a treatment, storage, disposal, or recycling facility and the signed receipt for this letter is the Department of Health Services acceptance of this affidavit. If this is not the correct procedure, please send us a written procedure to properly establish our facility as a Generator.

      I will call you next week to see if we can solve this problem as soon as possible.

Agency letter regarding misunderstanding.

Note: Letters to government offices have to be clear and concise—especially where toxic materials are concerned.

Toxic Substance Control Division
Region 3
1405 N. San Fernando Blvd., Suite 300
Burbank, California 91504

Dear Mr. _____ ,

Again we need your help. On October 21, 19____ , your office granted a variance from the Hazardous Waste Facility Permit requirements to (name and address of company), EPA ID #_____ . We are now being asked to pay a facility fee and to complete an Annual Facility Hazardous Waste Report. This problem has also rolled over to our (city) Aerospace Division at the same address which operates under EPA ID #_____ . Our status has not changed from Generator to TSDF Facility. This is an error.

Please look into this problem and advise us as to what steps are required to correct the records to reflect our status as "Generator."

Sincerely,

Letter trying to clear up misunderstanding with government agency.

Note: Follow-up is essential.

Dear Mr. _____ ,

Our flow meter was repaired as of May 1. Attached is a copy of the Instrument Calibration Report and the Flow Monitoring System Maintenance Record for your file.

If you have any questions, please call me at _____ between 8 A.M. to 5 P.M., Monday–Friday.

Letter to government agency regarding reports.

Note: When dealing with outside agencies, everything should be in writing.

January 19, 19____
Ref. No. PE: _____

Gentlemen:
    Attached is the blue copy of the Hazardous Waste Manifest, document number _____ as required by your office.

Letter replying to government request.
Note: This factual note is written solely to ensure that something is on the record.

Dear Dr. _____ ,

    Attached is a concept and drawing provided by (name), Product Engineer, of the electrolytic treater with one pass. Since there are no ESCA results for P_____ and P_____ , we can not discuss one-pass effect in detail at this moment. However, the following issues are of major concern:

    a. Fill yarn removal after electrolytic treatment

    b. Initial chemical reaction control for oxygen generation

    c. Electrode interval adjustment for oxygen content

    d. Effective length and width for new treater

    Please discuss these issues with your chemical engineers prior to the final design proposal.

Letter pertaining to design.
Note: Issues are clearly defined.

This is to confirm our telephone conversation about the results of the meeting held January 19, 19____ on your Phase II proposal attended by (name) and myself.

1. We would like a detailed calculation on the shell temperature at furnace temperatures of 1600 C in all four zones and another one at furnace temperatures of 1100/1250/1250/1350 C in the first, second, third, and fourth zones respectively.
2. Provide oxygen test ports at the inlet and outlet of the getting furnace.
3. The SCR and transformer cabinets to be separate from the controller (UDC 5000 On/Off switches and the other monitoring devices) cabinet.
4. Water cooling for the cabinets should be eliminated. Air conditioning is preferred.

Could you provide the answers to these questions within 30 days, or by March 12.

Letter follow-up to meeting with outside vendor.

Note: Problems are detailed and the return date is specified.

Dear _____ ,

On behalf of the (name) "team" who were privileged to visit the (name) facilities in (where), I thank you and your associates for a most informative and productive visit. In addition to being overwhelmed with your gracious hospitality, we were truly impressed by the fervor and commitment of everyone we met over the (name) Pursuit of Excellence. To witness the measurable results of years of dedicated effort by (name) employees to strive for continuous improvement and customer satisfaction was inspiring to us who are just beginning the creation of a Total Quality Management philosophy and environment at (name).

Again, (name), our sincere thanks to all of the (name) associates who made our visit so worthwhile. The (name) "associates" look forward to working with the "best supplier" in the textile business!

Letter thanking vendor for hospitality.

Note: A letter of this type is appropriate when two companies share expertise.

Purchase Order # _____

Account Number _____

March 29, 19____

Dear _____ ,

Enclosed herewith are 5 samples of carbon fibers for SEM analysis. Please do surface morphology (X6000) and cross section (X1200 and X6000) with 2 sets of photographs for the following:

1. RL154 (F)
2. P311-1
3. P312-1
4. P313-1
5. P341-0

Please analyze in the right manner and respond to the above request by submitting the test results to me on April 12, 19____ . Please ship via Federal Express Overnight Service.

Letter requesting analysis.

Note: The method of shipment is spelled out along with the due date and exact samples.

Purchase Order # _____

Account Number _____

Enclosed herewith are 5 samples of XRD (La, Lc d-space and B-orientate) for testing:

1. P310-9
2. P311-1
3. P312-1
4. P313-1
5. P314-0

Please analyze these samples in the right manner and respond to the request by submitting the test results to the undersigned by April 7, 19____ .

Letter requesting analysis.

Note: The materials submitted and the due date are spelled out clearly.

May 05, 19_____
Ref. No. _____

_____ , Ph.D.
Material Sciences Branch
(Company)
Chertsey Road
Sunbury-on-Thames
Middlesex TW 167LN

Dear Dr. _____ ,

    The first sample is (name) 46-8B (Run P321-0, 5 amps
[3.5 volts/loops]). Please analyze as soon as possible.

    The second sample is carbon fiber (unsized) from (name)
precursor (3rd-shipment, #_____). The surface treatment
was only ozone (0.3%, 95 C).

    We need results of these studies by June 10, 19_____ .

    Please analyze oxygen, content/functionality by (name). If
you should have any questions, please call me at (number).

Letter requesting analysis.

Note: The company lists the date when studies are needed. Deadlines are a must.

Just after we spoke today, I received a call from (name) accepting our offer of the Chief Engineer position here in (city). I plan on notifying you by phone but wanted to personally assure you (in writing) that I and the rest of the (city) staff think highly of you, your qualifications, and your personal bearing. The one overriding consideration in awarding this position outside the company was the desire to have an individual with experience in foreign operations. (Name) experience with (Company) in Indonesia coupled with a strong background in project evaluation and mine operations gave him the nod.

I know you and others at (company) may doubt our company's resolve to promote from within but I am certainly confident that someone with your background, abilities and determination will succeed with (company). And, with the rate at which we are planning to grow, the next opportunity will be soon.

I wish you the best when that opportunity arrives.

Letter to unhappy employee passed over for post.

Note: The specific reasons for the choice were given.

Dear _____ ,

I have known (name) for the past 18 months she has worked for the (name) engineering group as an engineering technician. Although she came to us with no formal experience in surveying or (name) engineering procedures in general, she has caught on extremely quickly and has in a short time become one of our most proficient field technicians. She has consistently performed these office and field duties with a positive, cheerful attitude even in the dead of Winter when the weather can be miserable in the pit.

In addition to her engineering technician contributions, (name) has on several occasions stood in for the (company) clerk, often with little advanced notice. Most noteworthy of her efforts here is that she was always able and ready to perform the wide variety of tasks I required in a prompt and proficient manner, even with a minimal amount of training. She also excelled in the difficult role of daily production accounting and in the frequent personal interface with the production foremen to ensure our production was being correctly reported.

I truly feel that she would make you a valuable and loyal employee. She has demonstrated to me a good working knowledge of the major administrative functions you undoubtedly seek and is an above average practitioner of the two most popular word processing and spreadsheet computer software packages.

If I can provide any additional amplifying information or answer any question you may have, please feel free to call.

Letter of recommendation.

Note: Specific accomplishments of employee are mentioned.

Some weeks ago, when you visited our facility, you mentioned that should we need your advice, you would be happy to return and spend a day at the plant examining the quality control procedures we have in place. Yesterday, I received word from the directors that on June 22, less than 30 days from now, the entire board would be visiting our plant and examining our QC methods.

We have been so occupied filling orders and working on various projects, we have, frankly, let QC slide. This is where I need your help. Could you spend a day or afternoon, with us and let me take you through our QC procedures? Afterwards, a critique on our methods would be greatly appreciated.

Frankly, I am quite concerned that we have let QC slide, and I am searching for some solid remedies, which I know we can get from your observations. Your expertise in the area is unparalleled and something every one of our facilities could utilize. I would greatly appreciate a visit, and I will call you next week to see how your schedule looks.

If you can, I, and all of us, would certainly owe you one!

Letter asking for favor.

Note: This letter requesting assistance from a colleague who has expertise in a particular area includes well deserved flattery.

Congratulations on your induction into (name of society), and welcome. Your outstanding achievements are something that everyone in our group knows of, and we are proud to have you as a fellow member.

Letter congratulating fellow engineer on indoctrination into society.

Note: Congratulatory notes do not have to be long, drawn out letters. The impact of a few sentences can be just as great as a page-long letter.

On behalf of all of us who attended the (name) conference, I would like to thank you for your outstanding presentation on "Travel Beyond the Internet." Your message was not only clear and to the point, but it was one of the most entertaining I have ever heard at a conference.

Once again, thank you for your participation and your contribution to the conference.

Letter to colleague complimenting them on presentation.

Note: Thanking a participant not only shows the speaker that they were appreciated, but it helps strengthen professional relationships.

(Name) has been on our staff as a structural engineer for the past four years, and during that time I have had the opportunity to work closely with her as well as observe her ability in the field.

(Name) has demonstrated a real team attitude, which shows in the high regard her fellow employees have for her. She has also demonstrated her technical skills on numerous projects that have been enormously important to our company. Her projects are always thorough and on-time.

Equally as important is (name) friendliness, work ethic, and problem-solving ability. Oftentimes, the group turned to her for solutions when we were temporarily stymied.

We're extremely sorry that her husband's company is moving, and I recommend (name) wholeheartedly for the position she is seeking.

If I can be of any further assistance, please call.

Letter of recommendation for employee.

Note: In today's corporate environment, any letter that goes out as a recommendation should go through human resources first.

Your presentation on "Robotics, the hidden ramifications," at the CISC Conference was powerful and intriguing. I have been working on many of the same concepts for the past few years, and have come up with several scenarios that our companies may not have thought about. They are events that could play an important role in the future of our industry.

I know your schedule is busy, however, I think it could benefit both of us, as well as our companies, if we could spend an hour or so together discussing some of the new research and development that has just emerged on the subject.

If your schedule permits, and you would like to explore the subject in greater depth, please give me a call.

Letter requesting a colleague collaborate on a project.

Note: Sharing information is something that not everyone likes to do. Thus, this note allows the recipient to take action, but only if he chooses. The writer could initiate the contact with a closing sentence that said something like "I will give you a call next week to see what your availabilities might be."

I would like to express my deep appreciation for having being chosen as the recipient of the (name) Engineering Award for 1914.

The award carries with it a great deal of significance, and needless to say I am thrilled to be the person chosen to carry the (name) banner for the next 12 months.

Thank you, once again, for this very special honor.

Letter of appreciation for being selected for an award.

Note: Thank-you notes never go out of style, and can be handwritten as well.

I was saddened to hear that you will be leaving our group, however, I am ecstatic for you and the new opportunity you have taken. I have thoroughly enjoyed working with you, and found your teamwork, cooperation, knowledge, and innovativeness second to none.

You have also been a splendid ambassador for our profession. Please accept my heartiest congratulations on your new assignment. You will be missed.

Letter or memo to someone that is leaving the organization.

Note: This can be a handwritten note, memo, or letter.

Effective this Monday, vacations must be taken between (date) and (date). In the past, we have given new employees a week's vacation during their first year even if they had not earned it by being here a full twelve months. If the employee left prior to the year being up, we charged back the unearned vacation time.

To eliminate the confusion caused by this policy, we have revised our vacations so that employees accrue vacation at the rate of one day every three months. Therefore, if you begin working on the first of January, at the end of March you would be entitled to one vacation day.

Employees who have been here for more than a year, will not be effected by this policy.

Memo to staff regarding vacation.

Note: Vacation policies should be clearly spelled out. This memo explains policies to new employees.

216

I was fascinated by your article on (subject) that ran in the BSEE Journal last month, and congratulate you on being chosen by the society to write it.

The study you cited was quite informative and the way you presented it was highly entertaining, a combination that one rarely finds together. Congratulations, and I certainly hope to be reading more from you in the future.

Letter to colleague congratulating them on article printed in Journal.

Note: Congratulatory notes can be handwritten for greater effectiveness.

Dear _____ ,

On behalf of (company name), I would like to offer you the position of Chief Engineer, reporting to me at the company headquarters in Albuquerque. This offer is subject to the following terms and conditions:

Starting Date

On or about June 12, 19____

Starting Salary

$_____ per annum.

Benefits

You will participate in (company) regular package of fringe benefits, a summary of which is attached.

Incentive Plan

You will be eligible to participate in the company incentive plan, which allows for you to earn up to an additional 40% of your base salary.

Vacation

We agree to grant you 1 week of vacation to be taken before the end of the 19____ . For subsequent vacation time you will start with five years service which will allow you to take 3 weeks per year starting in 19____ . Future vacation will be in accordance with company policy except that you will continue to retain the added five years of service for vacation purposes. With current policies, this means that 4 weeks of vacation which is normally earned after ten years of service will be afforded to you after your first five years with the company.

Temporary Living Expenses

Temporary living expenses for reasonable costs of meals and lodging will be provided for a maximum of 30 days.

Letter offering employment.

Note: This letter spells out all terms and conditions of employment.

Relocation

The movement of your household goods to Albuquerque will be provided by the company. If necessary, we will also provide up to 30 days of temporary storage of these household goods to allow you time to make permanent housing arrangements.

Sale of present home

You may sell your present home directly or through a broker, or may sell directly to (company name), our relocation company. If you elect to sell your home directly through a broker, (company name) will pay the broker's commission and other closing costs directly. You have the option to sell directly to (company name) at a sales price based on the average of two market appraisals that are within 5%. Normally you have 60 days to accept their offer during which time you may still sell your home directly or through a broker at a higher price.

We trust this meets with your approval. If the terms and conditions as outlined are acceptable, please sign one copy of the letter and return to me. If there are any questions that you have please call and discuss these with me as soon as possible.

Clark, all of us who met you here in Albuquerque are very pleased you have elected to join (company name) and we are anxious to begin working with you.

Sincerely,

_____

(your name)
(your title)

I understand and agree with the terms and conditions of my employment with (company name) as outlined above.

_____

Clark _____

Please accept the heartfelt condolences of everyone on the engineering staff for the loss of Dr. (name). During the five years he was here, we all became quite familiar with him and thoroughly enjoyed his morning coffee breaks and his amusing comments on the day's events.

If there is anything we can do for you or your family, please do not hesitate to contact us. Our thoughts and prayers are with you.

Letter of condolence.

Note: Condolence and sympathy notes should be handwritten.

It has been sometime since we had the opportunity to serve your company, and since that time we have introduced a number of innovations to our _____ unit.

Knowing your company's needs, I thought that some of these new developments would be of interest. I'll call you to see if we might get together in the near future so you can view some of them.

In the meantime, I hope all's well at _____ Company.

Sincerely,

Letter from engineering sales staff to a client.

Note: Follow-up notes should be part of every company's marketing plan. The note should come from the salesperson.

Thank you for giving me the opportunity to meet with you and members of your department yesterday.

I know (name) serviced your account for a number of years, and made many friends while doing so. While his presence will be missed, I would like to assure you and your staff that our company will continue to provide the same high quality service that has been our hallmark.

If I can be of any service, please don't hesitate to give me a call.

Sincerely,

Letter from new technical sales person to client.

Note: There should be a stream of contact and conversation between any new salesperson and a client.

I would like to take this opportunity to personally thank you for selecting our company to handle your information technology needs. I know you gave a great deal of thought prior to choosing our company, and we are extremely grateful for the confidence you have exhibited in our firm.

Although we service the latest in technology, we think of ourselves as a company that will always have a personal, as well as a technological, commitment to our customers.

If there is any question I can answer, please call. In the meantime, thank you, once again, for selecting _____ .

Letter from servicing department to new customer.

Note: Companies are attentive to prospects when they are pursuing business, but sometimes they forget to communicate with them afterwards. Frequent communication is a must, especially when a client relies on you.

Thank you for your recent inquiry into the software packages we currently have on the market.

I am enclosing a brochure and would like to point out that our software was recognized by _____ Weekly, as being on "the cutting edge of the industry for 1996."

We are also preparing a new package that will be introduced shortly. If you have any specific questions, please call me at (number). I look forward to hearing from you.

Letter to prospective client inquiring about products.

Note: The manufacturer not only communicates with the prospect, but tries to pique his interest with the mention of a new product.

Your letter of (date) inquiring about our biotech progress, has been brought to my attention, and I would like to thank you for your interest.

Our company has made significant progress in the _____ area, and our new product can be utilized to boost crop production more than 40%. At the same time, it has been deemed environmentally safe by the EPA, and given an unqualified endorsement by the FDA.

I would be happy to bring you through our facility for a demonstration. I will give you a call to see if we might arrange a mutually convenient time.

Thank you for your interest in _____ Genetics, and I look forward to meeting you.

Letter to prospect inquiring about new product line.

Note: The second from last paragraph is important because it mentions that the company will call the prospect. To be effective, all letters should be followed with telephone calls.

Thank you for opening an account with our firm. As one of the leaders in the genetics field, I can assure you that our products are not only state-of-the-art, but they have an exceptional high quality that we pride ourselves in producing.

Obviously, your firm's quality reputation is well-known, and we are enormously pleased that you have selected _____ as your supplier. I'd like to briefly set forth our terms, which _____ , our sales manager, may have mentioned. Invoices are payable within 30 days of receipt, with a 2% discount available if your payment is remitted within ten days of receipt. We have put this discount in place because we believe it is an excellent opportunity for our customers to increase their profit margin.

If I can help explain anything else relating to credit or delivery, please call.

Letter to client opening a new account.

Note: The company has the letter serve two purposes: (1) a welcome and (2) to reiterate the credit terms.

Congratulations on your appointment to (name). With your concern and abilities, I am sure your presence on the (organization) will make a significant difference in the growth and progress the (organization) makes in the future.

Once again, all of us at (company name) congratulate you and wish you the best as a member of (organization).

Congratulatory letter on election or appointment to specific office.

Note: When a client—or employee—is appointed or elected to a position of prestige, recognition by peers is always welcomed.

We discussed the past due amount on your account last Wednesday, and at the time you said the monies had been put in the mail the previous day. Although it has been nearly a week since our conversation, we have not, as yet, received any funds.

In view of that we are holding all shipments until a check arrives and the past due amounts are cleared. I regret to say that we cannot fulfill any new orders.

If a check has been mailed, please accept our thanks. If not, please call immediately so we can clear the matter up.

Collection letter.

Note: Collecting funds, especially from an account that has consistently said one thing and done another, is difficult. Although these letters should be diplomatic, they must be firm.

It is with regret that I must tell you we have had to change the credit policy on your account because of past due balances.

From now on a check must accompany each order for merchandise. This will be in force until your account has been brought up to date, and at that time we will reevaluate your status.

As one of our most valued accounts, we regret having to change policy and hope that this will not interfere with our long and profitable relationship. I look forward to resolving this matter as soon as possible. Please call me by next Wednesday so that we might discuss this and clear it up.

Collection letter to a valued account.

Note: A gentle but firm tone requesting payment.

Our companies have been doing business together for more than five years, and it is difficult for us to understand why you have not responded to the reminders we have sent about your past due balances.

If you are experiencing a problem, please call me immediately. We are anxious to retain the goodwill our companies have shared over the years. This note is not, incidentally, to request payment but rather to encourage you to call our credit manager to discuss your bill and any extension you might need.

Please let us hear from you soon.

Collection letter.

Note: Another gentle approach to requesting payment.

I am extremely pleased to tell you that we finished revamping our _____ PC line, and effective this Friday, we will be cutting our production time by one-third. That means, of course, that delivery of your goods will be that much faster, and with the same, high quality we have always provided.

I know you are in the midst of a busy season, but if you are in our neighborhood at any time, please let me know. I would like to show you through the new facility and give you a first-hand look at how we have been able to combine both speed and quality on a high tech production line.

Production letter communicating good news.

Note: This letter allows the company to let the customer know that their product or service is going to improve. Many times, firms do not let their customers know about improvements—and that is a mistake. Positive news helps build the company's image in the client's eyes.

As we near our fourth birthday, I am reminded by our accounting department that this will be the best year in our history. In fact, our production is up more than 18%, which is certainly gratifying to all of us here at _____ Industries.

Even more gratifying are clients such as your company, _____ . As I look through our records, I realize that you have been with us through most of our growth. That growth, as you know, was not always smooth, yet your company has always stood by our side.

As our birthday approaches, I would like to express our appreciation for your business and loyalty. And I would like to put another candle on the cake, in your honor.

Letter expressing appreciation of product support to client.

Note: Recognizing customer loyalty is never out of place.

For the past four years, our company has absorbed six different price increases without raising the cost to our customers. Last month, however, we experienced a raw material increase of more than 15% which, unfortunately, is causing us to raise our distributor and wholesaler prices.

Unfortunately, we could no longer forestall the inevitable. Our new price list is enclosed, and it goes into effect on June 1. Any orders, of course, placed between now and the first, will be processed at the old price.

I'd like to thank you for your valued business and courtesy in the past, and I hope you understand the reasons for the increases.

If you have any question, please call.

Letter explaining price increase.

Note: Price increases should be explained.

I can't remember ever having a more enjoyable evening than last Wednesday at the dinner you hosted for our department.

Thank you for inviting us to a most memorable evening.

Thank-you note for dinner.

Note: A formal note.

My sincere thanks to you and your charming wife for the enjoyable evening. The dinner was outstanding, and you both made us feel so comfortable that I am sure we stayed much longer than any of us realized. We enjoyed every moment.

Once again, many thanks to a wonderful host and hostess.

Thank-you note for more casual dinner.

Note: An appropriate thank-you note for an intimate dinner.

Your speech was extremely entertaining, informative and certainly enlightening. You covered so many areas, that I found myself identifying with each and every problem you mentioned. I especially enjoyed the point you made about today's production workers and how they differed from those just a few years ago. It was food for thought.

Thank you for sharing your valued experiences with so many of us.

Letter thanking a speaker.

Note: Sending a thank-you note mentioning a specific point to a speaker is always nice.

Chapter 7

Wrap-Up—Thirty-One Simple Tips and Rules

Even the best writers compose below average correspondence occasionally. The problem is usually either writing before thinking the message through, or writing the same as you speak. Taking a few minutes to organize your thoughts can solve the first difficulty, but the latter is more complex because writing is not the same as speaking. What we put on paper never looks or sounds like the same words that were spoken.

"That's not what I meant," is a familiar line spoken by many executives who were interviewed and then see their remarks in print. As Mark Twain said, "the difference between the right word and the almost right word is the difference between lightening and the lightening bug."

The written word does not carry the same inflection as the spoken word. The written word cannot convey the gestures that speakers utilize. Thus, many executives (and others who are interviewed) often feel that they were misquoted. Most of the time the speaker simply failed to grasp the difference between speaking and writing. Words can look dramatically different when they are written down.

The differences between the written and the spoken word can give new meanings to memos and letters. In school the difference was described as the distinction between "denotation," which is what a word actually means, and "connotation," the secondary or hidden meaning that a word has. When writing, keep the hidden meaning in mind. Does the word convey some thought that you do not want to pass on?

When examining a correspondence that just does not sound right, you will usually discover that it is one word or phrase that leads the reader astray. Editing will usually uncover this flaw.

The following is a list of 31 tips and rules to help improve your letter and memo writing.

1. *AIDA (Attention, Interest, Desire, Action).* The four principles of AIDA are behind any letter or memo. For ease of writing, put the four principals on a sheet of paper and list the points for each. Attention is usually only a sentence. Interest builds a case. Desire begins to show the reader the benefits. Action gives the reader a way to act.

2. *IBC (Introduction, Body, Conclusion).* IBC is the easiest of all letter/memo writing formulas. Think of the conclusion first. What point do you want to make? Write the conclusion and then the body. The body contains the evidence, facts, and information that support the conclusion. The introduction, which is usually just another way of stating the conclusion should be written last.

3. *The three "Ps" (personality, psychology, and politics).* When writing letters and memos keep all three "Ps" in mind. What is the personality of the recipient; the psychology behind the request; the political ramifications in the department or company?

4. *The boilerplate.* Most of the letters and memos in Chapters 5 and 6 are boilerplate. They can be adapted for dozens of other correspondence needs.

5. *The USP (Unique Selling Proposition).* Every good sales letter contains a USP. The USP sets your product or position apart. If a department is competing for more funding, the USP may be that the funding will go for a product or service that is a *greater potential revenue producer than any other that the company has in development.* USPs should be part of proposals and any documents trying to sell management, prospects, or customers on a product, service, or request.

6. *Double-spacing.* Letters are usually single-spaced. Letters that go beyond one page can lose their readability and their impact. Break up long letters into smaller paragraphs, bulleted items, and indented points. If you do set a letter single-spaced due to length, double-space between the paragraphs.

   Memos that go beyond three-quarters of a page also encounter readability problems. Long memos benefit from the bulleting technique, shorter paragraphs, and double-spacing.

7. *The place for emotion.* Letters or memos that are replete with emotional language and punctuation lose their impact. The reader gets accustomed to the emotional terms and does not pay attention to them. In some cases, the reader may even resent the words and the opinions of the writer. Sometimes an emotional word or term is necessary, but they should not be overused. Use emotional words for emphasis, and that normally means not more than once on a page. A correspondence that relies on emotion, rather than facts and logic, has a hard time selling the reader.

8. *Opinion-makers.* Every company has opinion-makers, and their approval on a correspondence adds validity. Any technical professional receiving backing for their argument or position from an opinion-maker will add credibility to their proposal and help the sale.

9. *The prose.* Letters and memos can be written in either formal or informal prose. Most letters can be written in an informal style. Informality helps convey meaning, and gives more feeling to the correspondence, a valuable ingredient when trying to sell someone with a letter or memo.

10. *Subject drift.* Letters and memos should cover only one subject. If discussing more than one topic is necessary in the correspondence, use a logical sequence. Do not drift back and forth between two subjects. If the letter or memo is going to cover a myriad of subjects, begin with a summary.

11. *Summary.* The summary is one of the most valuable paragraphs that a writer can utilize in a proposal. The summary is especially useful when the correspondence is longer than one page. A summary saves reader time, and helps get the message across.

12. *Conclusion.* Letters and memos must reach their conclusion. Do not leave the reader in a position where they have to decide what the conclusion is. Present both sides of a case (or argument) objectively, and draw a conclusion based on those facts.

13. *Action.* If it is the writer's responsibility to state the facts but not make the decision, the letter or memo should ask the recipient (decision-maker) for an answer or for action. Putting deadlines and dates in the correspondence will help guarantee a timely response.

14. *The one-on-one approach.* Even though a letter or memo may be addressed to numerous people, approach the correspondence

as if it is being written to one person. By focusing on one person—rather than a faceless group—writers make correspondence more effective, impactful, and personal. These characteristics are useful if you are trying to sell a point-of-view.

15. *Repetition.* Speakers will make a point, repeat it, and come back to it. That method works well with the spoken word, not in written correspondence. When writing a letter or memo, make your statement, prove it, and draw a conclusion, but do not repeat the same thing over and over. Repetition bores the reader.

16. *Typos.* Typos destroy the message and the credibility of the writer. Readers will assume that if "you do not care enough to spell it correctly, you must not care much about the message in the letter or memo."

17. *General vs. specific.* Generalities do not convince readers; specifics do. In correspondence, the writer can start off with a general statement, but must follow up with specifics that support the statement. Letters and memos consisting entirely of generalities will end up in the wastebasket.

18. *Length.* In today's fast-paced corporate environment no one has hours to spend reading letters and memos. Keep all correspondence as short as possible by writing in sound bite fashion.

19. *Assumptions.* Statements made in correspondence should be explained. Do not assume the reader knows what you mean.

20. *Strategy.* Always consider the goal of the correspondence before writing it. Is it informational? Does it seek a decision? Is it after support? Whatever the goal, a strategy should be composed to reach that goal. The strategy should contain numerous back-up and supporting points, that will lead the reader to the correct conclusion.

21. *The reader's needs.* Consider what concerns the reader has and address those needs. Show how the proposal or request will impact the reader.

22. *Frustration and anger.* Do not send correspondence when frustrated or angry. Any letter or memo composed in the heat of an argument will be packed with emotion, will contain few facts, and will turn off the reader. Write the letter or memo but hold it a day, reread it, and edit it.

23. *The lowest common denominator.* Consider all letter and memo recipients. Correspondence must be written in language that everyone reading it will understand. Not everyone within a company will understand technical terms.

24. *Adjectives.* Descriptive words are useful, but too many adjectives can give the reader the impression that the writer is not objective.

25. *Competition.* Letters or memos should not attempt to build a case by criticizing the competition. Recognizing competitors and their products and services is important, but using negative language in correspondence damages the message.

26. *Acronyms.* Use acronyms only when necessary and always explain them.

27. *Benefits.* Every letter and memo is selling something. Be sure to show the recipient the benefits of "buying" the proposal or product.

28. *Requesting funds.* Where does the money go? When requesting funds, make the argument for additional funding before stating the amount. Putting the dollar figure first can cause management to make a decision before hearing the logical arguments that are presented in the letter or memo.

29. *Word processors.* Thanks to word processing, letters and memos do not have to look as if they were typed on manual typewriters. With indents, bullets, and simple design changes, a letter or memo can have a look that will help keep the reader's interest.

30. *Dates.* Letters and memos should always be dated.

31. *Salutations and closings.* In today's market personalization is important, as is the correct spelling of the recipient's name and title. Salutations can take many forms, including these five impersonal ones:

Dear Sir:
Dear Madam:
Dear Ms:
Dear Sir/Madam:
To Whom It May Concern

If the recipient has a title it should be used:

Dear Dr. _____ :
Dear Professor _____ :

Dear Dean _____ :
Dear Senator _____ :
Dear Governor _____ :

Formal salutations:

Dear Dr. _____ :
Dear Mr. _____ :

Informal salutations:

Dear Joe:
Dear Candace:

Formal closings:

Yours very truly,
Very truly yours,
Respectfully,
Yours respectfully,

And less formal:

Best regards,
Sincerely,
Sincerely yours,
Cordially,
Yours cordially,

In today's business world, the line between formal and informal is thin. As a rule, letter and memo writers should utilize what makes them feel comfortable. Use formal closings for letters to people with whom you have little communication or whom you do not know.

Common sense is the heart of all correspondence. This book has provided many rules and techniques that will make letter and memo writing easier, but no ingredient has more impact on correspondence than common sense.

Common sense in combination with the tips and techniques in this book will help make your letters and memos more effective.

Index